CW00339183

Special Problems
in the Study of
Sufi Ideas

Books by Idries Shah

Sufi Studies and Middle Eastern Literature
The Sufis
Caravan of Dreams
The Way of the Sufi
Tales of the Dervishes: *Teaching-stories Over a
Thousand Years*
Sufi Thought and Action

**Traditional Psychology,
Teaching Encounters and Narratives**
Thinkers of the East: *Studies in Experientialism*
Wisdom of the Idiots
The Dermis Probe
Learning How to Learn: *Psychology and Spirituality
in the Sufi Way*
Knowing How to Know
The Magic Monastery: *Analogical and Action Philosophy*
Seeker After Truth
Observations
Evenings with Idries Shah
The Commanding Self

University Lectures
A Perfumed Scorpion (Institute for the Study of
Human Knowledge and California University)
Special Problems in the Study of Sufi Ideas
(Sussex University)
The Elephant in the Dark: *Christianity,
Islam and the Sufis* (Geneva University)
Neglected Aspects of Sufi Study: *Beginning to Begin*
(The New School for Social Research)
Letters and Lectures of Idries Shah

Current and Traditional Ideas
Reflections
The Book of the Book
A Veiled Gazelle: *Seeing How to See*
Special Illumination: *The Sufi Use of Humour*

The Mulla Nasrudin Corpus
The Pleasantries of the Incredible Mulla Nasrudin
The Subtleties of the Inimitable Mulla Nasrudin
The Exploits of the Incomparable Mulla Nasrudin
The World of Nasrudin

Travel and Exploration
Destination Mecca

Studies in Minority Beliefs
The Secret Lore of Magic
Oriental Magic

Selected Folktales and Their Background
World Tales

A Novel
Kara Kush

Sociological Works
Darkest England
The Natives Are Restless
The Englishman's Handbook

Translated by Idries Shah
The Hundred Tales of Wisdom (Aflaki's *Munaqib*)

SPECIAL PROBLEMS IN THE STUDY OF SUFI IDEAS

Idries Shah

ISF PUBLISHING

Copyright © The Estate of Idries Shah
The right of the Estate of Idries Shah to be identified
as the owner of this work has been asserted by them
in accordance with the Copyright, Designs and
Patents Act 1988.

All rights reserved
Copyright throughout the world

ISBN 978-1-78479-192-6

First published 1966
Published in this edition 2019

No part of this publication may be reproduced or
transmitted in any form or by any means, electronic,
mechanical or photographic, by recording or any
information storage or retrieval system or method now
known or to be invented or adapted, without prior
permission obtained in writing from the publisher,
ISF Publishing, except by a reviewer quoting brief
passages in a review written for inclusion in a journal,
magazine, newspaper, blog or broadcast.

Requests for permission to reprint, reproduce etc., to:
The Permissions Department
ISF Publishing
The Idries Shah Foundation
P. O. Box 71911
London NW2 9QA
United Kingdom
permissions@isf-publishing.org

In association with The Idries Shah Foundation

The Idries Shah Foundation is a registered charity in
the United Kingdom
Charity No. 1150876

THE TEACHER

People think that a teacher should show miracles and manifest illumination. But the requirement in a teacher is that he should possess all that the disciple needs.

Ibn el-Arabi

THE TEACHING

The purpose of Sufism is not to be what people imagine it should be – but to help in the attainment of the real destiny of man.

Hasan of Basra

THE TAUGHT

This present life of yours is a stage, an alighting point. A halting-place is for rest from the journey, refreshment in company, effort in preparation for the future. If you do not know the facts, you need to know them soon. Tomorrow could be too late.

Hilali of Samarkand

Contents

Preface

IN THE TWELVE years since this monograph was first published, the explosion of interest in Sufi ideas has shown no sign of abating. Perhaps the most striking development has been that people no longer believe that Sufism is 'a little Persian sect', or 'ecstatic Mohammedan mysticism'. Reference to the ever-increasing research and publication on the subject has supplied so much information that the Western (and often the Eastern) categories are clearly seen not to fit the subject at all. If it is 'little', how has it had millions of adherents? If it is 'Persian', why are most of its participants outside Persia? If it is a sect, of what is it a sect? If it is ecstatic, how is it that Sufi authorities condemn ecstaticism as often as they approve it? If it is Mohammedan, how is it that certain of its greatest authorities deny this? Only information can combat incorrect statements of 'fact'.

Even more uncomfortable for the pedants who believe that they had definitively labelled Sufism are the questions of its contributions to world culture and knowledge. Those who have claimed that the Sufis are selfish or world-denying have had to be reminded of the work and words of such classical masters as Saadi: 'The Way is none other than in the service of the people.' Those who write and speak of Sufism in terms of morbid religiosity have been hard put to account for its humour and broad-mindedness. Those, again, who have tried to represent it as derivative of, say, Christian mysticism have been reminded that a not insignificant amount of Christian material has been shown to be derivative from the Sufis. In the literary field, critics and others have been fascinated to see how the Sufis, over the centuries, have infused their tales and their spirit into what had been thought of as national literatures. In sociology and anthropology, Sufi work has more recently been seen as prefiguring work done in modern times by Western workers. The same is true of both philosophy and psychology: where Sufi writings testify to important influences upon, or anticipations of, areas of current interest.

But we must not forget the cultists. They have continued to ransack the Sufi tradition for materials to support their own weirdery. Hence references to extra-terrestrial matters have been disinterred with delight; Hafiz has been discovered as a book for taking omens, gaining as many adherents in some places as the *I Ching*. References to vegetarianism, or what are imagined to be such, have been received with rapturous delight. Indications of Extra-Sensory Perception and 'psi' abilities, torn out of context, have been eagerly adopted.

Yet the fact that people will assume that anything of interest is useful and relevant to their own preoccupations should, of course, only be seen as evidence of a certain disposition of the human mind. If, tomorrow, all the people of the West, or many of them, adopt Islam, it will be established that Sufism is, in fact, Islam. If, as is still the case, people rest upon the basis of what is considered to be a Christian culture, they will look for 'real Christianity' in Sufism. If flying saucers are 'real', passages from the Sufis will be invoked to prove by hindsight that they were referred to therein. If their existence is disproved, the same texts will be interpreted to refer to something else.

All this, of course, goes to show that 'things mean what I want them to mean' is a standard human posture. Until what the things really do mean becomes the commanding principle, the student will not be able to profit from them in a learning sense. This distinguishes between the entertainment and instructional function. The issue is clear: Sufism, like many another way of knowledge, can either be employed for purposes of recreation – to confirm existing beliefs and to give emotional stimulus – or else one can learn from it. One cannot shift from one of these modes into the other until one has learnt how to shift. People who need the psychological prop are not primarily learners, they are often in need of therapy first. Sufism is not a therapy, it is a teaching.

The foregoing facts make it very easy for the Sufi to deal with the sensationalist or intellectual; just as easy as it is for the sensible to deal with the foolish: and just as difficult. The sensible person says: 'We must distinguish between fact and opinion.' When he says this, he is effectively dealing with whoever does not make such distinctions. That is to say, he has laid down verifiable parameters about these two things. This does not mean, of course, that he can get the idiotic to accept his statement. But he has dealt with him, enabling third parties to see both the rationality of the sensible man and the possibility that something may be learnt from him by adopting his stance. The sensationalist, on the other hand, may well not accept the distinction, because there is often more satisfaction for him in maintaining his symptoms: in seeking and obtaining emotional stimuli.

The emotionalist, here, may clearly be seen to resemble the specialist in any field. Like the specialist, his area of attention is limited, and his preoccupations are correspondingly specialised. The professor of literature, coming to Sufism, wants to find literary material; the aesthete, aesthetic material; the religionist, faith and practice.

Even an ordinary reading of the Sufi writings of the past, including much which I have translated and published during the past fifteen years, shows how deeply aware Sufis have been of this problem, and how they have tackled it. Sufism, they have insisted, is not there for people to adopt pieces of it which appeal to them, in the order and manner which pleases them. It is there to be learnt, by its own methods and in the order and manner which the Sufi phenomenon itself requires.

In this respect the Sufi Way resembles every other form of teaching or body of knowledge. The fundamental aim of education, after the acceptance of the fact that it is needed, is that it shall be brought to the student in accordance with the nature, capacity and character of the student: and that what is brought to the learner shall be in the manner, at the level and through the knowledge of the subject which is required by the subject.

It is interesting to note that few people dispute these requirements. But it is not agreement which is needed, but performance. The student should not think that he or she automatically understands and accepts the principles. It is necessary to think and to act in accordance with this acceptance.

Failure to observe these simple rules would make it almost impossible to learn anything. Those who find this hard to follow need only imagine trying to learn mathematics, say, according to their own rules or curriculum; or trying to learn the alphabet only through working with the letters whose shape pleases them.

Therefore it is sad but true that it must be stressed that Sufism, like any other study, has its own, intact and comprehensive, body of knowledge, its own teachers and its own methods. These exist because the Sufis are adepts at their subject and know how to teach it. They are not in need of help in formulating teaching-systems – neither are they people who have stumbled across something and have to be investigated to establish the meaning and rules of what they do, through the efforts of third parties.

I do not mean to say that most people imagine that the Sufis are indeed primitive or ignorant people of this kind. I do find, like the masters of the past, that a large number of people actually behave as if this were so. Now this problem of the unrecognised assumption motivating the attitude of the would-be learner is a problem within the learner which has to be overcome or dissolved before learning can take place. It is not the blind leading the blind, but the blind trying to lead the sighted.

An analogy would be that of the student of, say, French, who wanted to work out what French was and what parts of it might suit him by questioning and studying a French teacher. The teacher would, almost certainly, draw his or her attention to the basic error of the approach. Sufism is there to be learnt. Its teachers are there to teach. The learner must have as correct an attitude towards learning as the teacher has knowledge and competence. If these facts are not established, there can be no real learning; and the consequence is that the only intake by the alleged learner can be emotional stimulus or fragmentary bits and pieces.

For those who are statistically minded, it may be repeated that a study of no less than seventy thousand questions and conversations has shown that the basic difficulty of people of all cultures in acquiring higher knowledge is precisely this: that they do not approach it as if it were knowledge at all, but as something to heal them, or to answer the question of the moment, or to stimulate them in what can only be called a reactional manner. For this reason I have dealt with the matter in detail in my *Learning How to Learn* (London 1978, 2017).

The problem exists, of course, because of social conventions. What has happened is that, in most if not all cultures, certain assumptions are made about social situations. The basic one which is made in social groups is that all the participants are in some way qualified for membership of the group because they have been admitted to it. Now this is a wholly admirable posture and belief if we are dealing with a group established for emotional stimulus or interchange. It is positively harmful to make the assumption in a learning situation; being equivalent to assuming that an illiterate 'has every right and every capacity' to read a book. If you insist upon this, you will be acting against the interests, if not the mistaken self-esteem, of the illiterate.

Special Problems in the Study of Sufi Ideas, because of the foregoing facts, has had an influence upon its readers in accordance with their existing attitudes, psychological desires and information-stock. Hence, its information content has stimulated the desire for more information from those who desire this intake. It has produced disagreement from those who have already the ingrained desire to disagree (as well as from those who may have better grounds for dissent). It has stimulated emotionally those who put a premium upon this. It has aroused great admiration among those who want to admire, quite apart from whether it contains anything admirable. And it has been understood by others. It has, therefore, fulfilled its role, and continues to do so: for in our field there are many bonuses to be obtained from one and the same impact. You can gain information and stimulate the desire to have more; you can have real feelings verified and less appropriate ones revealed to you. If the reader seeks the reinforcement of pre-existing prejudices, he can obtain this almost anywhere. It is sad to note how often our materials are employed for this very subjective purpose when so much more accessible material abounds, and when there are so many people who would be only too delighted to get the attention which the dissentients choose to level at those not interested in controversy.

Idries Shah
London 1978

Theories about Sufism

LET US PRESUME no background of Sufi ideas on the part of an imaginary student who has recently heard of Sufism. He has three possible choices of source-material. The first would be reference books and works written by people who have made this subject their especial province. The second might be organisations purporting to teach or practise Sufism, or using its terminology. The third could be individuals and perhaps groups of people, not always in Middle Eastern countries, who are reputedly Sufis. He may not yet have been induced to believe that Sufism is to be labelled 'Mohammedan mysticism', or 'the cult of the Dervishes'.

1

What does this man learn, and what are his problems?

One of the first things that he could discover is that the very word 'Sufism' is a new one, a German coinage of 1821.[1]

No Sufi ignorant of Western languages would be likely to recognise it on sight. Instead of 'Sufism', our student would have to deal with terms such as 'The Qadiris', named after the founder of a certain rule, who died in 1166. Or he might come across references to the 'People of Truth', 'The Masters', or perhaps 'The Near Ones'. Another possibility is the Arabic phrase *Mutassawif*: 'he who strives to be a Sufi'. There are organisations called 'The Builders', 'The Blameworthy' which in constitution and sometimes even minor symbolism closely resemble Western cults and societies like Freemasonry.[2]

These names can ring oddly, and not always felicitously, in the contemporary Western ear. This fact alone is a real, though not obvious, psychological problem.

As there is no standard appellation for Sufism, the enquirer may turn to the word *Sufi* itself, and determine that it suddenly became current about one thousand years ago,[3] both in the Near East and in Western Europe;[4] and it is still in general use to describe particularly the best product of certain ideas and practices, by no means confined to what people would conventionally call 'religious'. He will find plenty of definitions for the word, but his problem is now reversed; instead of coming up against a mere label of no great age, he gets so many descriptions of *Sufi* that he might as well have none at all.

According to some authors, and they are in the majority, *Sufi* is traceable to the Arabic word, pronounced *Soof*, which literally means 'wool', referring to the material from which the simple robes of the early Moslem mystics were made.[5] These, it is further claimed, were made of wool in imitation of the dress of Christian anchorites who once abounded in the Syrian and Egyptian deserts and elsewhere in the Near and Middle East.

But this definition, plausible though it may appear, will not solve our problem as to name, let alone ideas, in Sufism. Equally important lexicographers stress that 'Wool is the garb of animals'[6] and emphasise that the Sufi objective is towards the perfectioning or completing of the human mind, not to emulate a herd; and that the Sufis, always highly conscious of symbolism, would never adopt such a name. Furthermore, there is the awkward fact that, according to tradition, the Companions of the Bench[7] – the *Ashab as-Safa* – are said in tradition to have been the Sufis of the time of Mohammed (who died in 632) and that they formed themselves into an esoteric group in the year 623, and that their name is a derivation from this phrase. Although some grammarians have pointed out that the 'wool' origin is etymologically more likely – and more probable than, say, the derivation from 'piety' (*Safwa*), or even *Saff* (contracted from the phrase 'First Rank of the Worthy'), others have contested such opinions on the ground that nicknames do not have to abide by the rules of orthography.

Now the name is important as an introduction to the ideas, as we shall see in a moment. Meanwhile let us look at its associations. Sufis claim that a certain kind of mental and other activity can produce, under special conditions and with particular efforts, what is termed a higher working of the mind, leading to special perceptions whose apparatus is latent in the ordinary man. Sufism is therefore the transcending of ordinary limitations.[8] Not surprisingly, in consequence, the word *Sufi* has been linked by some with the Greek word for divine wisdom (*Sophia*) and also with the Hebrew cabbalistic term *Ain Sof* (the absolutely infinite). It would not reduce the problems of the student at this stage to learn that it is said, with all the authority of the *Jewish Encyclopaedia*, that Hebrew experts regard the Cabala and the Hasidim, the Jewish mystics, as originating with Sufism or a tradition identical with it.[9] Neither would it encourage him to hear that, although the Sufis themselves claim their knowledge to have existed for thousands of years, they deny that it is *derivative*, affirming that it is an equivalence of the Hermetic, Pythagorean and Platonic streams.[10]

Our still uninitiated student may by now be thoroughly confused: but he has had a glimpse of the problems of studying Sufi ideas, even if only because he can witness for himself the unproductive struggle of scholastics.

A possible refuge would be found if our man could accept the affirmation of a specialist – Professor Nicholson – or if he asked a Sufi.

Now Nicholson says: 'Some European scholars identified it with Sophos in the sense of "theosophist".[11] But Nöldeke... showed conclusively that the name was derived from *Suf* (wool) and was originally applied to those Moslem ascetics who, in imitation of Christian hermits, clad themselves in coarse woollen garb as a sign of penitence and renunciation of worldly vanities.'[12]

This characteristic, if not venturesome, opinion was published in 1914. Four years earlier, Nicholson himself had offered his translation of the 11th century *Revelation*, the earliest available Persian treatment of Sufism, and one of the most authoritative Sufi texts. In its pages the author, the venerable Hujwiri, specifically states, doggedly translated but ignored by the Professor, that *Sufi* has no etymology.[13]

Nicholson shows no curiosity about this claim: but thinking about it could have led him to an important idea in Sufism. For him, quite clearly, a word *must* have an etymology. Unconsciously assuming that 'no etymology' must

be absurd, he looks no further in that
direction but, all undismayed, continues to seek an etymological derivation.
Like Nöldeke, and many others, such a
mind will prefer the word 'wool' to the
seeming paradox of 'no etymology'.

This is surely the reason why, in his
recent book on Sufism, the learned
Dominican Father Cyprian Rice (an
admirer and pupil of Nicholson)
says, half a century after the English
publication of Hujwiri's text – a version
which he praises: '...from their habit of
wearing coarse garments of wool (*suf*)
(they) became known as Sufis.'[14]

But acquaintanceship with Sufis,
let alone almost any degree of access
to their practices and oral traditions,
could easily have resolved any seeming
contradiction between the existence
of a word and its having no ready
etymological derivation. The answer

is that the Sufis regard the *sounds* expressed in writing by the letters S, U, F (in Arabic the signs for *Soad*, *Wao*, *Fa*) as significant, in this same order of use, in their effect upon human mentation.

The Sufis are, therefore, 'the people of SSSUUUFFF'.

Having disposed of that conundrum (and incidentally illustrating the difficulties of getting to grips with Sufi ideas when one thinks only along certain lines), we immediately see a fresh and characteristic problem arising to replace it. The contemporary thinker is likely to be interested in this explanation – this idea that sound influences the brain – only within the limitations imposed by himself. He may accept it as a theoretical possibility in so far as it is expressed to him in terms which are regarded as admissible at the time of communication.[15]

If we say: 'Sounds have an effect upon man, making it possible, other things being equal, for him to have experiences beyond the normal,' he may persuasively insist that, 'This is mere occultism, primitive nonsense of the order of Om-Mani-Padme-Hum, Abracadabra and the rest.' But (taking into account not objectivity but simply the current phase of accepted thought) we can instead say to him: 'The human brain, as you are doubtless aware, may be likened to an electronic computer. It responds to impacts or vibrations of sight, sound, touch and so on, in certain predetermined or "programmed" ways. It is held by some that the sounds roughly represented by the signs S, U, F are among those for reaction to which the brain is, or may be, programmed.' He may very well now be able to assimilate this wretched simplification into his existing pattern of thinking.

This condition existing in our *vis-à-vis*, the special problem here is that many of those who are anxious to study Sufi ideas are in fact unwilling, because of a systematic intellectual commitment, to allow certain contentions about Sufism, held by Sufis, to be retained in the mind. This situation, whose existence is demonstrated by much personal experience, is far more widespread than this single example might suggest.

The problem is not made easier by the common tendency of the individual addressed to attempt to deal with Sufi ideas by outright rejection. A typical answer goes something like this: 'To think in the terms suggested by you would wreck my established ways of thought.' This individual is quite mistaken in believing this: to the Sufi he is really a man under-valuing his own capacities. Another reaction is to try to rationalise or reinterpret the ideas being offered him in the terms of some system (anthropological, sociological, sophistical, psychological) which he himself finds more to his taste. In our example this subjective condition would perhaps be expressed in the statement: 'Ah, yes, this theory of the influence of sound has obviously been produced in order to give a more esoteric twist to the rather mundane fact – wool.'

But this kind of thinking will not ultimately succeed because, far from being represented only among primitive tribes or buried in books in dead languages, Sufi ideas are in varying degrees contained in the background and studies of up to forty million people alive today: those connected with Sufism.

Limitations of Contemporary Approaches to Sufism

A LARGE PART of this problem is the powerful tendency in the present day to place all people, things, ideas, into specialist categories. Categories may be all very well – and who could do without them? – but when any matter is being studied and there is only a limited choice of label offered, the experience can seem like being told by Henry Ford that 'You can have any colour automobile, providing it is black.' This problem which the enquirer is possibly even unaware of (his preoccupation with a few categories) is matched by that of the Sufi in attempting to convey his own ideas under other than ideal conditions.

Here is an illustrative example, chosen from recent experience. I give it because it will incidentally, and not in a forced 'system', tell us something about Sufi ideas.

In a recent book[16] I mentioned, among much else, that Sufi ideas and even literal texts were borrowed by or lay behind theories, organisation and teachings of such diverse aspect as those of Chivalry, of St John of the Cross,[17] St Teresa of Avila,[18] Roger Bacon,[19] Geber, the father of Western alchemy[20] – surnamed 'the Sufi' – Raymond Lully the Majorcan,[21] Guru Nanak[22] the founder of Sikhism, and the *Gesta Romanorum*,[23] as well as Hindu Vedantist teachings.[24] Certain deteriorated psychological procedures, too, have passed into the Western literature of magic and occultism,[25] as well as legitimate psychological ideas and processes, sometimes thought of as recent discoveries.[26]

This book created, among reviewers and others, a quite remarkable and manifold reaction.[27] Some were enthralled, not always for good reasons; but it is the others of whom I am speaking. What I had done was to collect the results of whole lifetimes of other people's academic research, often buried in monographs and seldom-read books, always by highly respected Orientalists and specialists of one kind or another. I also included 'live' material from Sufic sources. But, although the quoted material was by no means a complete selection from the teachings available, it was too rich a mixture for some readers. And yet many of them should have been far more familiar than I was with work already done in their own fields. One celebrated expert had uncomplimentary things to say about me, to say nothing of those who attacked what they only *thought* they found in my work!

Shortly after this phase, in conversation with a certain 'specialist', I mentioned that not only had I been relying in my thesis upon such authorities as Professors Asín, Landau, Ribera, Tara Chand, Guillaume and others of equally unimpeachable integrity, but that I had in my own text freely quoted their names and works; and that in other cases I had quoted the books by such ancients as Lully, Bacon, Geber, and others who mentioned the Sufis by name, Sufi books, or Sufism specifically. His reaction was not to agree that the experts should have known their job better, but to repeat the name of my main critic. Settling back in his armchair and chuckling, he said: 'You've got him, my boy. Make your choice: do you just want to discredit him, or do you want his job?'

My 'error', as far as treatment of the subject was concerned, had simply been that instead of quoting authority and building up, step by step, an unassailable 'case', I had assumed that the book would be read thoroughly and that the facts would speak for themselves.

My friend in the armchair automatically assumed that I was engaged in a game of displacement of someone in authority. The original critic had propelled himself into the attack on an equally false assumption: that I lacked good material because I had not hammered it home triumphantly enough.

What is perhaps more astonishing, when we look at problems in the study of Sufi ideas, is the treatment given to them by people who, if not experts in 'the field' itself, might have familiarised themselves with the academic resources available. Hence, to take an instance of a not uncommon trend in the West,[28] we find a Professor writing a book on philosophers of the East, in which, out of nearly one hundred thousand words, only about three hundred (one page out of over three hundred) are concerned with the Sufis. And this in spite of the fact that the same author had published a work on the philosophers of the West:[29] both types of thinker having been influenced by Sufi sources. This influence is never mentioned. The redoubtable English philosopher Bertrand Russell, too, is found to have written a huge book, *Wisdom of the*

West,[30] in which Western thinkers whose connection with Sufi thought is clear are named, but where no mention of Sufis or Sufism may be found.

It may be said that both of these books are popularisations intended for the general reader: but they do, after all, carry the names of scholastics, and they do lack information.

General readers, or members of the non-Orientalist disciplines, consulting these books, would have little means of knowing what had been left out.

Quite revealing among the problems facing anyone who wants to study Sufi ideas is the constant repetition of unproved theories, represented as facts, by 'specialists' and others who themselves have little objectivity.

Since Sufic study is carried out mainly by direct methods (and it has been known to be conveyed entirely by gesture, symbol and demonstration), when we lose this element in our study, relying upon books, we must be at the mercy of those who advance all kinds of subjective theories.[31]

There are those who say that Sufism is developed from historical Islam; and they include some Sufi apologists writing in this vein for good reasons. Some say that it is the reverse: a reaction against Islamic attitudes. There are those who would believe that its ideas stem from Christianity as they know it; or that they are partially or wholly attributable to the effect of Persian dualism; or from China, or India; or again, non-Indian. There are champions of the Neoplatonic theory, of Shamanism – and we could extend this list. The picture starts to look like one of people debating whether iron comes from Sweden or Japan.

We may call Sufi ideas 'a psychology', not because this term adequately describes Sufism, but because nowadays 'wisdom' is not a popular word. It is to be noted, however, that because the dictionary-makers do not understand us, the possibility of Sufi ideas being understood is not thereby excluded.

In the problem of permissible categories of study we see that Sufism straddles many of them. We can find materials bodily taken from Sufism, ideas which are characteristic of it, methods, tales, legends and even poetry of the Sufis in the phenomenon of the Troubadours,[32] in the William Tell legend of Switzerland,[33] in the Near Eastern cult of the 'Peacock Angel',[34] in Gurdjieff[35] and Ouspensky, and Maurice Nicoll, the Swede Dag Hammerskjöld,[36] Shakespeare,[37] in the psychology of Kenneth Walker,[38] in the tales of the Dane Hans Christian Andersen,[39] in the works by Sir Richard Burton (himself a Qadiri dervish),[40] in a recently issued series of textbooks on learning English from the Oxford University Press,[41] in contemporary children's books,[42] in the religion of the 'witches',[43] in the symbology of the Rosicrucians,[44] of the Illuminati,[45] in many mediaeval scholastics of the West,[46] in the Bhakti cult of the Hindus, though this is much popularised in the West as a traditional Hindu system,[47] in the secret books of the Ismailis,[48] in the organisation, name and techniques of some of the so-called Assassins,[49] in tales and techniques of supposedly Japanese Zen origin,[50] or reputedly connected with Yoga,[51] in material relating to the Knights Templar,[52] in psychotherapeutic literature, in Chaucer,[53] and Dante Alighieri[54] – and I am only enumerating the sources almost at random.

Misunderstandings of Sufi Ideas and Formulations

WHAT IS A Sufi idea, how is it expressed, where do we look for it? Many ideas we can easily identify as being derived from the Sufis because of context or actual attribution in the text. But the special problem beyond this is that there is no record of any other body of ideas or system which has penetrated so widely and so far into so many departments of life and thought, in the East and West. No mind has been trained to expect such a thing, except that of the Sufi, who does not need the material. As a consequence we get this questioning: is Sufism a series of shamanistic cults, a philosophy, a religion, a secret society, an occult training system, the mainspring of whole ranges of literature and poetry, or a military system, a chivalric, or perhaps a commercial, cult?

Serious problems in locating genuine and relevant Sufi ideas and practices exist, too, for any student who has already met a watered-down, generalised or partial variety of Sufism, whether in the East or the West. There are many hundreds of people in Europe and America who perform 'dervish dance, whirling or turning', though it is specifically on record in easily accessible literature[55] that this practice was especially 'prescribed' *for local reasons*, by Rumi for the people of Asia Minor, the region of Iconium.[56] In a similar way, when those influenced by the Western 'work' or 'system' which attempts to follow Gurdjieff[57] and Ouspensky[58] – and there are thousands of them – are forthrightly told that their exercises and methods are well known and applied in certain Sufi schools, but that they are to be used in a different way and more intelligible manner corresponding to the community involved, they are – more often than not – incapable of assimilating this statement. The Sufic gains in such cases are beginning to be overwhelmed by the losses due to misunderstanding or misapplication.

Another, and until recently a rapidly growing, phenomenon making use of some Sufi ideas and practices, is known to thousands in the West as 'Subud'. Its procedure is mainly based upon Naqshbandi-Qadiri[59] methods, but in its current presentation these have been turned upside down. In the Subud meeting called the *Latihan*, the member waits for certain experiences, believed to be the working of God within him. Some are slightly affected, some profoundly, some not at all. The interesting thing here is that the Subud attitude values the experience, and many people who are not affected or who cease to perceive it, drift away. The remainder are stalwarts of the movement. But, according to Sufi ideas and practice, it is precisely those who do not feel subjective states, or who have at one time been affected by them and no longer feel them, who may be real candidates for the next stage.[60] To the Sufi, one who does not know this may appear like a man trying to exercise his muscles, who thinks the exercises are no good because he no longer feels stiffness in his limbs. The gains of 'Subud' are offset, at least in part, by the losses.

This is the real problem in the attempted study of the original Sufi ideas through such popularisations.[61] As this inversion has invoked Sufi terminology, the student may very well not be able to shed the Subud associations when he approaches Sufism.

Yet another problem, strongly characteristic of Sufism, awakens a great deal of opposition. This may be stated by saying that Sufi literature contains material which is ahead of its time. Certain Sufi books, some translated into Western languages and therefore a matter of verifiable record, contain material which seems to become comprehensible only when 'new' psychological and even scientific technical discoveries are

made and well-known. A verification
of claims which once seemed bizarre
or impossible then becomes possible.
Western Orientalists and others have
noted, for instance, that the Afghan
sage Jalaludin Rumi[62] (died 1273),
Hakim Sanai of Khorasan[63] (14th
century), El-Ghazali of Persia[64] (died
1111), and Ibn el-Arabi of Spain[65]
(died 1240), speak of psychological
states, theories of psychology and
psychotherapeutic procedures which
would have been incomprehensible
to readers without the 'infrastructure'
of knowledge which has lately been
acquired in the West. These ideas are
called 'Freudian' and 'Jungian' and so
on, in consequence.

Sufi claims that 'man rose from the
sea', and that he is in a state of evolution, covering an enormous period
of time, appeared to be fanciful

nonsense until the 19th century Darwinists seized upon this material with delight.[66]

References said to be to the forces contained in the atom,[67] to a 'fourth dimension',[68] to relativity,[69] to space travel,[70] telepathy, telekinesis, are frequent; sometimes as facts, sometimes as due to techniques, sometimes as man's present or future capacities. Accounts of precognitive awareness and other phenomena of this kind are to be judged only in the light of comparatively recent knowledge or still await verification by conventional scientists. Over seven hundred years ago, Ibn el-Arabi stated that thinking man was forty thousand years old, while scholastic Jewish, Christian and Moslem belief was still committed to scriptural 'datings' of the Creation being only four to six thousand years before. Some recent research, however, now dates 'modern' man to about thirty-five thousand years ago.[71]

Some of the greatest and most 'learnedly ignorant' ridicule to which Sufis have been subjected, still maintained in some circles, is due to their having stressed in their classics the dangers of obsessions being implanted in people. Sufis for centuries have pointed out the undesirable nature of indoctrination and emotion being confused with spiritual gifts, to the horror of religious enthusiasts. Only in the past few decades, almost, have other people come to know better than the clerics.[72]

The especial secondary problem here, too, is that although the scientist will, rightly, await verification of this material, or try to investigate it, gullible occultists will pursue the Sufi who speaks of these things as deriving from Sufism, urgently demanding, as of right, magical knowledge, self-mastery, higher consciousness, hidden secrets and the rest.

For the Sufi, these trustful and sometimes unbalanced people can be more of a problem than the sceptics. The believers create a further problem because, baulked of easy magical knowledge, they may quite quickly turn to those organisations (well-meaning and otherwise) which seem to them able to satisfy this thirst for the unknown or the unusual: or offering 'short-cuts'. It is not to be denied that we use this phrase – but always with qualifications: 'Adepts have, however, devised shortcuts to an attainment of a knowledge of God. There are as many ways to God as there are souls (selves) of men.'[73] Several such bodies exist in Britain and America. If you write for the literature of one of them, for example, you may receive a publication in which it is claimed that Sufis prefer a vegetarian diet and that students must be 'free of caste, colour and creed', before developing 'occult powers'.

Other movements, using the name Sufi, idealise their founders, giving members a sort of inter-religious ceremony. More than one practises musical recitals supposed to throw the seeker into an advantageous ecstasy: in spite of the fact that Sufi teaching is widely on record that music can be harmful[74] and that it is what is taught, not the teacher, which is the point of Sufism. The gains in Sufi information are once more offset by losses due to faulty practice and selectively biased reading.

Asiatic immigration – Arab, mainly from Aden and Somaliland, India and Pakistan – into Britain has introduced another form of 'Sufism'. This centres around groups of Moslem religious zealots who gather for communal prayer-exercises which stimulate them emotionally and sometimes have a cathartic effect. Using Sufi terminology and similitudes of Sufi organisation, these have branches in many industrial and seaport cities of Britain.

The problem here is not only that many of the participants will not now be able to study Sufi ideas (since they believe that they already know them) but that just anyone – sociologist, anthropologist or ordinary member of the public – cannot always know that this does not represent Sufism: any more than American revivalist snake-handling represents Christianity, or the game of 'Bingo', mathematics. The gains, once more, are on a low level; the losses are not slight.

Like their indoctrinated confrères throughout the Moslem world from Morocco to Java, these coteries are often in reality groups of fanatics using the Sufi form. Some are plainly hysterics. Others never have heard of any other form of Sufism.[75] To them such claims as that of Ibn el-Arabi: 'Angels are the powers hidden in the faculties and organs of man' would seem utter blasphemy – and yet they revere Ibn el-Arabi![76]

It is not impossible that these entities (through sheer enthusiasm, efficient deployment of money and recourse to modern mass-publicity methods) will become generally considered by observers to be real

Sufis or representative of Sufi ideas. It is probably true to say that religion is too important a matter to leave to speculative non-expert intellectuals or clerics. The latter tend to 'scramble' devout activity. This is an ancient error. Ghazali was once believed in the West to be a Catholic theologian of the Middle Ages. 'St Jehosaphat' has been shown to be Buddha, and 'St Charalambos' of the Greeks has been revealed as none other than the dervish master Haji Bektash Wali, who founded the Bektashis.[77] The 15th century Christian saint Therapion is the dervish poet Turabi.[78]

Such developments can already be seen in countries of the East where enthusiasts, often pleasant enough characters, out-shout the Sufis, maintaining that their own antics are the true Sufism. This, in turn, has posed a sore and largely unrecognised problem for many Westerners interested in the Sufi heritage. Faced with acceptance or rejection, convinced that this must be Sufism because so many people locally consider it to be so, numbers of these students have reacted either by revulsion or by total, uncritical acceptance. In Britain, to say nothing of other Western countries, there are examples of the 'Sufi conversion syndrome' – sometimes in the case of not inconsequential persons, ready to leap into print to 'prove' that this cult, as they have seen it among ecstatic sentimentalists, is something to be adopted in the West.[79]

It can give one an almost uncanny sensation to compare this state of affairs with a hypothetical situation in an underdeveloped area where advanced ideas have penetrated but – through lack of accurate and appropriately systematised information – have been adopted by the local inhabitants in a superficial or untoward manner. One is tempted to think in terms of the 'cargo cults'[80] among less advanced communities, whose members built tin-can replicas of aircraft, believing that they could thus magically reproduce the wonders of supply of good things from the skies.[80A]

And yet there is no real lack of basic information on Sufi ideas. There is information, but much of it is not studied and assimilated by those who could do so. There is another characteristic problem here; the problem caused by the places where the material appears.

Much material on Sufism and the Sufis, some of it the product of excellent observation, enquiry and fieldwork in

Asia, Africa and Europe, appears from time to time in the general-circulation press. But because the work is not always by 'recognised specialists', or because it sees the light of day in media which are not regarded as authoritative in 'the field', it can be missed.

Here are a few recent examples:

In two brilliant articles in *Blackwood's Magazine*[81] in 1961 and 1962, O. M. Burke described the ideas and practices of Sufis in Pakistan, Tunisia, Morocco and elsewhere. He outlined theories and exercises well-known in Sufi practice but not always literally represented in its overt literature. In 1961, a Delhi newspaper[82] carried a good report of Sufi beliefs and deliberations in Paris. In a specialised scientific journal in 1962[83] there was an important contribution by an Egyptian physician in which ideas and psychotherapeutic procedures of a Central Asian dervish community with international ramifications were delineated. None of this material will ordinarily be quoted in Orientalist, or even occultist, literature.

No citation seems yet to have been made from an important article by another worker dealing with the living, oral tradition of 'secret teaching' in the Middle and Far East, which was published in the *Contemporary Review* in 1960.[84] The desire to diffuse Sufi ideas and practices and the special manner in which this is done, and also symbolic demonstrations of Sufi ideas carried out in a large Hindu-Kush community which has branches in Europe, provides another first-class document. Because, no doubt, it was published in *The Lady*,[85] a woman's weekly magazine, this could be considered lost as research material.[85A]

A resolute correspondent of *The Times* of London,[86] writing in 1964, imparted an account of ideas and practices in Afghanistan and their ramifications in the Arab world. It seems unlikely that this valuable report will ever form a part of the formal literature on Sufism. An article in *She* magazine in 1963, and another in September 1965,[87] contained at least some material of interest and some previously unrecorded facts.

Forms of Sufi Activity

WHAT ELSE DO the Sufis teach, how do they do so, and what special problems does this study pose for those who would wish to learn from a reputable source of the ideas?

The Sufis state that there is a form of knowledge which can be attained by man, which is of such an order that it is to scholastic learning as adulthood is to infancy. Compare, for instance, El-Ghazali: 'A child has no real knowledge of the attainments of an adult. An ordinary adult cannot understand the attainments of a learned man. In the same way a learned man cannot understand the experiences of enlightened saints or Sufis.'[88] This, for a start, is not a concept which would instantly commend itself to the scholar. This is no new problem. In the 11th century, Mohamed el-Ghazali (Algazel) who saved the Moslem theologians by interpreting Islamic material in such a way as to defeat the attack of Greek philosophy, informed scholastics that their mode of knowledge was inferior to that gained through Sufi practice. They made him into their hero, and their successors still teach his interpretations as orthodox Islam, in spite of his stating that the academic method is insufficient and inferior to real knowledge.

Then there was Rumi, the great mystic and poet, who told his audiences that like a good host he gave them poetry because they demanded it: providing what was asked for. But, he continued, poetry was tripe compared with a certain high development of the individual. Nearly seven hundred years later he could still sting people with this kind of remark. Not long ago a reviewer in a reputable British newspaper was so affronted by this passage (which he found in a translation) that he said, in effect, 'Rumi may think that poetry is tripe. *I* think that *his* poetry is tripe in this translation.'

But Sufi ideas, in being put in this manner, are never intended to challenge the man, only to provide him with a higher aim, to maintain his conception that there may be some function of the mind which produced, for instance, the Sufi giants. Inevitably, the contentious collide with this idea. It is because of the prevalence of this reaction that Sufis say that people do not in fact *want* the knowledge that Sufism claims to be able to impart: they really seek only their own satisfactions within their own system of thinking.[89] But the Sufi insists: 'A short time in the presence of the Friends (the Sufis) is better than a hundred years' sincere, obedient dedication' (Rumi).

Sufism also states that man may *become* objective, and that objectivity enables the individual to grasp 'higher' facts. Man is therefore invited to try to push his evolution ahead towards what is sometimes called in Sufism 'real intellect'.[90]

Sufis contend that, far from this lore being available in books, a great part of it must be personally communicated by means of an interaction between the teacher and the learner. Too much attention to the written page, they insist, can even be harmful. Here is a further problem: for it appears to oppose the scholar no less than the member of the vast modern literate community who feels, if at times only subconsciously, that all knowledge must surely be available in books.

Yet Sufis have worked long and hard to adapt the written word to convey certain parts of what they teach. This has led to the use of manipulated and enciphered materials: not designed especially or always to conceal a real meaning, but intended to show, when decoded, that what on its outward face seemed like a complete poem, myth, treatise and so on, is susceptible of another interpretation: a sort of demonstration analogous to a kaleidoscopic effect. And when Sufis draw diagrams for such purposes as these, imitators merely tend to copy them,[91] and use them at their own levels of understanding.

Another Sufi technique provides a further problem. Many Sufic passages, even whole books or series of assertions, are designed to stimulate thought, even sometimes by the method of arousing healthy criticism. These documents are only too often taken by their literalist students as faithful renderings of beliefs held by their original authors.[91A]

In the West in general we have plenty of translations. Mostly they are literal renderings of only one facet of multidimensional texts. Western students actually know that the internal dimensions exist, but they have not yet applied them to any extent in their work. To be fair it must be said that some have admitted that they cannot do this.[92]

Another Sufi idea, producing a problem which many have found it impossible to integrate in their minds, is the Sufi insistence that Sufism can be taught in many guises. Sufis, in a word, do not stick to any one convention.[93] Some quite happily use a religious format, others romantic poetry, some deal in jokes, tales and legends, yet others rely on art-forms and the products of artisanship. Now, a Sufi can tell from his experience that all these presentations are legitimate. But the literalist outsider, however sincere he may be, will often testily demand to be told whether these Sufis (or this and that group of Sufis) are alchemists, members of guilds, religious maniacs, humourists,[94] scientists – or what. This problem, while it may be special to Sufism, is by no means new. Sufis have been judicially murdered,[95] hounded out of their homes, or had their books burned, for using non-religious or locally unacceptable formulations. Some of the greatest Sufi classical authors have been accused of heresy, apostasy, even political crimes. And today they still come under fire from all kinds of committed circles, not just religious ones.[95A]

Even a cursory examination of reputed origins in Sufism will reveal that, although Sufis claim that Sufism is an esoteric teaching within Islam (with which it is therefore regarded as entirely compatible) it also stands behind formulations which many people consider to be quite different from one another. Hence, while the 'chain of transmission' of named teachers extends back to the Prophet Mohammed in this or that line of attribution used by a school or teacher, it may also be referred to – by the same authorities – as stemming from such as Uwais el-Qarni (died in the 7th century) who never met Mohammed in his life.[96] The authoritative Suhrawardi, in common with (though much before) the Rosicrucians and others, specifically states that this was a form of wisdom known to and practised by a succession of sages including the mysterious ancient Hermes of Egypt.[97] Another individual of no less repute – Ibn el-Farid of the early 13th century (1181–1235) – stresses that Sufism lies behind and before systematisation; that 'our wine existed before what you call *the grape and the vine*' – the school and the system:[98]

We drank to the mention of the Friend Intoxicating ourselves, even before the creation of the vine.

There is no doubt that dervishes, would-be Sufis, have traditionally collected together to study whatever remnants of this teaching they could find, awaiting the moment when an exponent might appear among them and make effective the principles and practices whose active meaning was for them lost. This theory is to be found in the West, of course, in Freemasonry (with its concept of the 'lost secret'). The practice is duly confirmed, for instance, in the textbook *Awarif el-Maarif*[99] and it has been regarded by those interested in such things as an indication of the occurrence of a messianic-expectation characteristic in Sufism. However that may be (and it belongs only to a 'preparatory phase', not to Sufism proper) there is evidence that people in Europe and the Middle East, whatever their psychological commitment of faith, have from time to time been located and inspired in the Sufi doctrines by teachers, sometimes of mysterious origins, who came among them. These people have for centuries been referred to as Universal, or

Completed, Men (*Insan-i-Kamil*). Such was the case with Rumi (13th century) and Shams of Tabriz; of Bahaudin Naqshband,* in the 14th century in Bokhara; of Ibn el-Arabi, who taught in terms of religion, figures of antiquity and love-poetry; and of many others less known in Western circles.

The problem for the student here may be not whether this 'irrational' form of action or refreshment of a tradition took place or not: it is the psychological difficulty of accepting such people as really having any special function to 'reunite the beads of mercury' or to 'reactivate, awaken, the inner current in man'.

---

*   Incorrectly but frequently rendered as 'Naqshiband'.

But we have not even started to enumerate the fields in which Sufis and entities known to have been devised by them (these latter being a minority of the real number, because Sufism is action, not institution) have carried out social, philosophical and other forms of action, in the past thousand years. Characters as seemingly diverse as the forthright Rumi, the saintly Chishti, the 'God-intoxicated' Hallaj,[100] the statesmen of the Mujaddids, have worked for centuries to further the actual reunification of communities seemingly irrevocably parted.

For their pains, and again assessed by the inadequate and often inaccurate standards of their commentators, these people have been accused of being secret Christians, Jews, Hindus, apostates and sun-worshippers. When the Bektashis used the number twelve, and gave, like Arabi and Rumi, Christian myths a high place in their teachings, it was (and still is) assumed that they only were capitalising on the local abundance of Christians deprived of effective leadership. The validity of this charge awaits the verification of the Sufi answer that Christian, and numerous other, formulations, contain a valuable measure of insights which, under suitable circumstances, can be applied to man.

The followers of Haji Bektash (died 1337) were and still are in some places regarded as immoral simply because of their practice of admitting women to their meetings. Nobody could, or would, understand them when they said that it was necessary to redress the social balance of a society based upon male supremacy. 'Social reinstatement of women' simply sounded, until

it recently became a 'respectable'
objective, like a cloak for orgies.

Nobody of consequence, even in the
19th and early 20th centuries, bothered
himself to look at the claim, made by
such as the distinguished Turkish Sufi
and savant Ziya Gökalp,[101] that Sufi
writers centuries ago had outlined and
employed theories later identified with
the names of Berkeley, Kant, Foullée,
Guyeau, Nietzsche and William James.

This brings us to another important
Sufi projection, one which causes
bafflement – and even rage – in certain
types of person, but which should
instead be faced. It is the assertion
that when Sufic activity becomes
concentrated at one point or in one
community in a very active and 'real'
(not imitation) form, it does so only
for a limited time and for distinct
purposes. It is the type of person who

says 'I want it here and now or not at all' who dislikes this statement. Put in another way, the idea is that no society is ever complete, neither are its needs exactly the same as those of other societies. No Sufi sets up an institution intended to endure. The outer form in which he imparts his ideas is a transient vehicle, designed for local operation. That which is perpetual, he says, is in another range.

Difficulties in Understanding Sufi Materials

IN THIS AGE of creeping institution-alisation it is at least as difficult as it has ever been to make this point effectively. Yet a thousand years ago the dervish wanderer Niffari in Egypt, in his still-influential classic the *Muwaqif* ('stops'), energetically stressed the danger of mistaking the vehicle for the objective.

Coming closely on the heels of this problem is the one of guidance or teachership. The Sufi teacher is a conductor, and an instructor – not a god. Personality-worship is forbidden in Sufism.[102] Hence Rumi: 'Look not at my exterior form, but take what is in my hand'; and Gurgani: 'My humility which you mention is not there for you to be impressed by it. It is there for its own reason.'[103] Yet such is the attraction of personality to the ordinary man that the successors of Sufi teachers have tended to produce, rather than a living application of the principles taught, hagiographies and bizarre and deficient systems. The theme of the temporary nature of the 'cocoon' is conveniently forgotten. Hence the constant need for a new exemplar.

A further problem for the student who is not aware of the above situation is the existence of what have been called 'illustrative biographies'. These contain material designed for study, to cause certain effects, much in the way in which myths can contain dramatised fact. With the passage of time they outlive their usefulness, and are then taken as lies or, alternatively, as records of literal truth. Where is the historian who will willingly relinquish such source-material? Hence, for example, because in a biography of Maulana Jalaludin Rumi[104] he is stated to have spent long periods in his Turkish bath, seekers of higher consciousness and would-be illuminates have actually been known to endow this report with such significance as to build and frequent their own steam-baths. They have, in turn, their own imitators...

Those who remember their nursery rhymes may be able to grasp one aspect of Sufic study by thinking about the unfortunate Humpty-Dumpty. Like Humpty, Sufi ideas have had a great fall – when they have been adopted at their lowest level. They have, in consequence, fallen in all sorts of strange places. Looking at the pieces of Humpty, we can call the emotionalists and conventional scholars 'the King's horses' and 'the King's men' of the rhyme. Like them, there is an inevitability about their helplessness to deal with the problem. A man and a horse – or any number of them – belonging to a king or otherwise, are suitable for just so many tasks, no more. Something is missing, as in the nursery rhyme: and, unless they are Sufis or use Sufic methods, they 'cannot put Humpty together again'. They have the horses, and they have the men; but they have not got the vehicle, the knowledge.

If Sufi ideas, as expressed in books and among preparatory or 'orphaned' communities, and given shape by the teachings and existence of a human exemplar, are in fact designed to produce a form of mentation more valuable than mechanical thought, the student might argue that he is entitled to know about the product. He may expect to find avowed Sufis taking an invariably significant or even decisive part in human affairs. While the Sufi would not accept that public acclaim is what he seeks (most of them flee it), and is not anxious to become a sort of Albert Schweitzer-cum-Napoleon-cum-Einstein, there is nevertheless massive evidence of the powerful Sufi heritage. More surprising than that, for those who seek to label and limit Sufism as simply this or that cult, is the extent and variety of the Sufi impact, even setting aside the Sufi claim that their greatest figures are almost always anonymous.

During the periods of mainly monarchical rule over the past millennium,

Sufis in the East have been kings or stood behind them as advisors. At the same time, under other conditions, Sufis have worked against the very institution of kingship, or to mitigate its abuse. The names of many of these men and women are well known. The Mogul Dara Shikoh of India sought to form an esoteric bridge between his Hindu, Moslem and other subjects.[105] Sufi patriots have fought against foreign tyrants, just as Sufi soldiers have fought for the preservation of existing states – sometimes on a grand scale, as with the Sufi-inspired Janissaries of Turkey, the resistance leader Shamyl of the Caucasus, the Senussi of Libya, or the dervishes of the Sudan. Almost all the literature of Persia in the classical period is Sufic, and so are innumerable scientific, psychological and historical works.

The citations just made are a matter of historical record, and could be greatly increased in range and number.

Whereas the fragmentary researches of committed scholars upon which I have often drawn in this discourse have their inestimable value in the preservation of fact, it remains for a new spirit of learning to assemble and collate the extent and value of the Sufi activity in human society. In this way we may preserve the gains and reduce the losses.

Such students – and here is another problem – in addition to being less prone to indoctrination than their predecessors, would have to take into account the contention of the Sufis themselves, when they say: 'Sufism must be studied with a certain attitude, under certain conditions, in a certain manner.'[106]

Many people, unthinkingly in too many cases, have rebelled against this dictum. But is it, after all, so very different from saying: 'Economics must be studied with a certain attitude (the desire to understand) under certain conditions (the discipline of scholasticism and the right books) in a certain manner (following a curriculum devised by those who know the subject properly)'?

The study of Sufism cannot be approached, for instance, from the single standpoint that it is a mystical system designed to produce ecstasy and based on theological concepts. As a Sufi poem by Omar Khayyam states:

> In cell and cloister, in monastery
> and synagogue:
> Here one fears hell, another
> dreams of paradise.

But he who knows the true
   secrets of his God –
Has planted no such seeds within
   his heart.[107]

It seems unlikely that much progress towards the widespread understanding of Sufi ideas will be made until more scholars avail themselves of Sufi interpretative methods. If they do not, they will continue to waste effort on secondary phenomena. This, in turn, poses a special problem for the Sufi himself. As Ibn el-Arabi has said: 'The Sufi must act and speak in a manner which takes into consideration the understanding, limitations and dominant concealed prejudices of his audience.'[108]

The correct study of Sufi ideas depends upon the supply and right use of the literature and also the contact with the Sufi instructor.

As to supply of literature, time may put that right in the ordinary course of events, although two recent experiences indicate that the losses, again, may be serious.

One of my books was criticised by an eminent scholastic and expert on Sufism in the Middle East on the ground that Mulla Nasrudin the joker was no Sufi instruction-figure. He did not know at the time, and perhaps still does not know, that at that moment a European student was actually living in a dervish community in Pakistan which was using Mulla Nasrudin and nothing else, as instruction material. An account of these studies was recently published in a British journal of religion.[109]

But merely adding to the information on Sufism is not enough. Not long ago, when I was innocently enquiring about holiday prospects from a Western intellectual whom I buttonholed on a Greek island, he rounded on me with a fair amount of abuse. Brandishing a copy of one of my own books, he said: 'You are wasting your time thinking about a holiday, and trying to waste the time of a man who is reading this book: something more important than all your holidays!'

Example of Sufi Ideas from Jalaludin Rumi (1205–1273)

MAN IS THE product of evolution. He continues this process. But the 'new' faculties, for which he yearns (generally unknowingly) come into being as a result of necessity. In other words, he now has to take part in the development of his own evolution. 'Organs come into being as a response to necessity. Therefore increase your necessity.'

When he does not realise this, man is in a state which is referred to as 'sleep'. He has to 'wake up'.

There is a means of doing this, but the means is not through scholastic endeavour and what man takes to be the exercise of intellect. The means is by what is called the 'direct perception of Truth'.

Man's thinking pattern is in the ordinary way based upon alternation and changes of mood. He needs what is conceived of as a unification of mentation.

Man's perceptions are faulty, because they are subjective and relative. They are also 'conditioned', so that he interprets things according to limited, not objective, standards. He may therefore be said to have little capacity for real judgement.

There are realms of mind far beyond the ordinary state of man. These advanced realms cannot completely be rendered in the language of the brain as it stands.

Because of these limitations, man needs the guidance of one who knows more.

The methods used to help in the production of the higher state of perception include historical, religious and fable frameworks, as well as exercises of all kinds.

All such formulations are 'ways'.

Men have warped and made useless these 'ways' by repetitiously insisting on literal meanings for the figurative. Thus are 'idols' made.

When man reaches behind exterior form, he can see that such forms, apparently multiple, stand before one and the same thing.

These teachings were given by ancient sages, and by Moses, Jesus and Mohammed. They have been changed and used in a minor and inefficient way.

This changing process is due to the use of man's vanity, where, for instance, he imagines that he can conceive more than he can at any given moment. As a result, giving a name to an undefinable concept makes him think that he has mastered it; or can master it, through having named it.

Beyond the confines of outward religion, man cannot truly call himself a Jew, a Christian, a Moslem. Ritual and dogmas have no place in this sphere.

Man can be conceived as incomplete, a 'limb severed from a body'.

The effort of man to reunite with the understanding from which he is cut off can be called 'the religion, or duty, of Love'. But this is not a religion as such things are normally understood by man.

The 'eye', the advanced organ of perception of that from which man is cut off in the normal way, is within man.

External impressions 'condition' man, so that he is insensitive to inner impressions.

Any 'language' (terminology) may be used to refer to the transformation of man. This is why such conventions as the language of alchemy are used; or the language of myth and fable, which often refers to psychological processes, not to historical events.

Those who have developed the 'higher perceptions' sometimes have to conceal this fact, for social and other reasons, behind a locally acceptable façade.

Some Assessments of Contemporary Sufi Writing

Representative English-Language, Urdu, Arabic and Spanish items

1. ABBAS, Sayed KHALIFA, 'This Man....', *Alsahafa* (Khartoum), 4 Dec 1972
2. *AFGHANISTAN NEWS*, 'New Book Covers Important Afghan Contribution to World Philosophy and Science', May 1964 (official publication)
3. A. H. C., *The Field*, 'Persian Sage', 22 Apr 1971
4. ALDISS, BRIAN W., 'The Mulla's Joke Book', *Oxford Mail*, 3 Nov 1966
5. ALLEN, TREVOR, 'The Subtleties...', *Books & Bookmen*, Aug 1973

6. *AMERICAN SCHOLAR, THE* (Review of *The Sufis*), Spring 1970

7. *ANDEAN AIR MAIL* (Lima, Peru), 'Idries Shah', 26 May 1972

8. ANDERSON, PAUL E. (Amer. Inst. for Continuous Educ.), 'Sufi Studies', *Library Journal*, Mar 1974

9. *ARGENTINISCHES TAGEBLATT*, 'Sufi-Buch-Ausstellung', 25 Nov 1972

10. AUSTIN, ANN, 'Teachings', *Tribune*, 23 June 1972

11. BANFE, CHARLES, 'Oriental Approaches to Life', *Peninsula Living*, 26 Sep 1970

12. BEALES, IAN, 'Bedtime Book of the Year', *Western Daily Press*, 7 Nov 1967

13. BELCHER, DAVID, 'Here is some good news on Oil', *Orange Enterprise and Journal* (Orange, Mass.), 12 Dec 1973

14. BLACK, WALTER, 'The Diffusion of Sufi Ideas in the West', *Univ. of Denver Quarterly*, Summer 1972

15. BODEN, P. K., 'Great Thinkers on Tape', *Times Educational Supplement*, 6 Apr 1973

16. *BOOK EXCHANGE*, 'Caravan of Dreams', June 1971

17. *BOOKS & BOOKMEN*, 'The Dermis Probe', July 1970

18. BOOTHAM, MICHAEL, 'Destination Mecca', *Books & Bookmen*, May 1969

19. BROOK-WHITE, S., 'Dervish Assembly in the West', *Siraat* (Delhi), Jan 1 1961

20. BUKHARI, ABDEL-AZIZ, 'International Symposium on Afghan Thinker', *Kabul Times* (Afghanistan), 4 March 1973

21. *CAPITAL, LA*, 'Lo que un Pajaro Debena Parecer' (Rosario), 31 Dec 1972

22. CASEY, JUANITA, 'The Way that you do It', *Irish Press*, 16 Jan 1971

23. *CHOICE* (Assn. of College and Research Libraries), Chicago, 111. 'Sufi Studies', Apr 1974

24. *CHURCH TIMES*, 'Thinkers of the East', 26 Feb 1971

25. *CHURCH TIMES*, 'East is East', 24 Nov 1967

26. CLARKE, ARNOLD, 'The Volcano of Achievement', *Dict. of Internat. Biography Mag.*, July 1970

27. *COLORADO ALUMNUS, THE*, 'The Diffusion...', Dec 1972

28. CORKE, HILARY, 'The Exploits...', *The Listener*, 15 Dec 1966

29. *DAILY EXAMINER* (Huddersfield), 'Exploring the Common Ground', 15 July 1971

30. *DIA, EL*, 'Cuentos de los Derviches', *La Plata*, 18 Feb 1973

31. E. C., 'A Fable of Today', *Evening News*, 16 Jul 1969; 'Do these Supermen Exist?', *Evening News*, 10 Feb 1969; 'Making the East Less Mysterious', *Evening News*, 1 Apr 1969

32. *ENCOUNTER*, 'In the World, Not of It', Aug 1972

33. ENRIGHT, D. J., 'Wise Heads, Wise Tales', *Encounter*, Dec 1970

34. *EVENING NEWS*, 'Beguiling', 27 May 1971

35. *EVENING NEWS*, 'Going Back a Bit', 24 Sep 1969

36. *EVENING NEWS*, 'The Odd Ideas we have about Islam', 17 July 1974

37. *EVENING NEWS*, 'Squire Shah', 12 Feb 1973

38. *EVENING STANDARD*, 'Meet the Mulla', 3 July 1973

39. FLYNN, BARRY, 'Proverbial Wisdom', *The Irish Press*, 10 Dec 1966; 14 Oct 1967; 14 Aug 1970

40. FOSTER, WILLIAM, 'The Family of Hashim', *Contemporary Review*, May 1960

41. GARVEY, J. C., 'The Book of the Book', *Irish Independent*, 5 Dec 1970

42. GILL, ANDY, 'Caravan of Dreams, etc.', *DARTS* (Univ. of Sheffield), 20 June 1974

43. GRIGSON, GEOFFREY, 'Neat Wisdom from the Near East', *Country Life*, 21 Nov 1968

44. GRIGSON, GEOFFREY, 'Reflecting with the Dervishes', *Country Life*, 26 Oct 1967

45. *GUARDIAN, THE*, 'Idries Shah, inventor, member of learned societies...', 8 Jan 1975

46. *GUARDIAN, THE*, 'Consider the Elephant', 26 Nov 1970

47. HALL, W. E., 'A Humorous Masterpiece', *Birmingham Post*, 26 Nov 1966

48. HILL, DOUGLAS, 'Teaching Stories', *Tribune*, 16 Aug 1968; 'Sufi Teaching', 24 Jan 1969; 'In Brief', 12 June 1970; 'From all Directions', 5 Feb 1971

49. *HINDU, THE* (see item 109)

50. *HINDUSTHAN STANDARD*, 'Oriental Wisdom', 4 Jan 1970 (Delhi)

51. *HINDUSTAN TIMES* 'Idries Shah', 18 Apr 1971 (Delhi)

52. HUGHES, TED, 'Secret Ecstasies', *The Listener*, 29 Oct 1964

53. *IMPRINT*, 'Meet the Author', Sept 1967 (Bombay)

54. *INDEPENDENT PRESS-TELEGRAM*, Long Beach California, 'The Way of the Sufi', 1 Jan 1970

55. 'JOHN LONDON', 'The Book of the Book', *Evening News*, 13 Nov 1969

56. *KABUL TIMES*, 'UNESCO International Book Year', 11 Feb 1973 (Afghanistan)

57. *KABUL TIMES*, 'Anthology of Afghan Stories now as Paperback', 13 May 1973 (Afghanistan)

58. *KABUL TIMES*, 'Idries Shah Honoured', 29 Nov 1970 (Afghanistan)

59. *KENT LIFE*, 'Looking at Books', Oct 1970

60. *KENT & SUSSEX COURIER*, 'Author Honoured', 18 May 1973 (Notebook)

61. *KENT & SUSSEX COURIER* ('Warwick Diary'), 'Books of the Year', 3 Jan 1969

62. *KILID-I-SIHAT* (Lahore), 'Idries Shah: Thinker, Researcher...', Apr 1973

63. *KING'S GAZETTE*, Journ. of King's Coll. Hosp., 'Book Reviews', Winter 1972

64. *KIRKUS REVIEW*, 'Tales of the Dervishes', 5 Nov 1969

65. KREK, MIROSLAV, 'Tales of the Dervishes', *Library Journal*, 1 Sep 1969

66. LANG, WALTER, 'A Book to Read Between the Lines', *Evening News*, 22 Jul 1970

67. LANG, WALTER, 'Who *Can* Change Human Nature', *Evening News*, 3 Mar 1971

68. LANG, WALTER, 'Folk Tales and Science of our Evolution', *Evening News* (London), 5 Apr 1972

69. LESSING, DORIS, 'Sinking Ships', *New Statesman*, 25 Nov 1966

70. LESSING, DORIS, 'An Elephant in the Dark', *Spectator*, Sep 1964

71. LESSING, DORIS, 'An Ancient Way to New Freedom', *Vogue*, 15 Sep 1971

72. LESSING, DORIS, 'Some Kind of a Cake', *The Observer*, Jan 1969

73. *LISTENER, THE*, 'Wise Words', 15 July 1971

74. *LITORAL, EL*, 'La antigua sabiduria en la calle Florida' (Concordia), 10 Apr 1973

75. MAHASSINI, DR ZEKI EL-, 'Idries Shah: the Philosopher, Writer and Poet...Illustrious Afghan of the 20th Century', *Asda* (Beirut), July 1971

76. *MAN* (South Africa), 'The Way of the Sufi', March/May 1969

77. 'MANDRAKE', 'Tapping Goodwill with Tape', *Sunday Telegraph*, 4 Feb 1973

78. MARTINEZ, HUMBERTO, 'La Comunicacion Directa e Intuitiva', *Diorama Excelsior* (Mexico), 9 Sep 1973

79. McWILLIAMS, CAROLE, 'Psychologist Claims Western Man Uses Only One Half of His Brain', *Boulder D. Camera*, 28 Apr 1973

80. *METHODIST RECORDER* ('Thinkers of the East'), 18 March 1971

81. M. F., 'Enchanted Tales', *The Irish Times*, 17 Dec 1966

82. MORENO, ARTHUR, 'Idries Shah: A Mind that has no Match', *Blitz* (Bombay), 9 Mar 1974

83. *NACION, LA*, 'Semana Internacional....', 29 Nov 1972

84. *NATIONAL HERALD MAGAZINE* (Delhi), 'Window on a New World', 25 Oct 1971

85. *NAYA PAYAM* (Pakistan), 'Sayyed Idries Shah', 12 Jan 1973

86. NAYYAR WASTY, PROF. HAKIM, 'Great Thinker Sayed Idries Shah', *Niyaz* (Pakistan), January 1973

87. *NEW SOCIETY*, 'East meets West', 22 Aug 1974

88. *NEW SOCIETY*, 'Teaching Stories', 20 June 1968; 'The Sufi Bite', 15 April 1971

89. *NEW YORKER, THE*, 'Talk of the Town', 24 Feb 1973

90. *NEW YORK TIMES BOOK REVIEW*, 'Books by Idries Shah', 7 May 1971

91. *NOVA*, 'The Short Story Classics/Paradise of Song, by Idries Shah', Feb 1970

92. *OBSERVER, THE*, 'Beyond Words', 18 Jan 1970

93. OLIVER, DOUGLAS, 'A Golden Anecdote', *Cambridge News*, 28 March 1969

94. *OPINION, LA*, 'Semana del Libro...', 30 Nov 1972

95. ORNSTEIN, PROF. ROBERT E., 'Intuition', *Intellectual Digest* (New York), Nov 1973

96. *OXFORD UNIVERSITY EXAMINATION PAPERS*, Honour School of Modern Languages, Trinity Term 1965, 18 June 1965

97. *PENTHOUSE*, Nov 1972

98. PANSHIN, ALEXEI, 'The Future in Books', *Amazing*, June 1973

99. *PAULA*, Review (Santiago de Chile), 'Fatima la Hilandera', 3 Oct 1974

100. *PSYCHOLOGY TODAY*, 'Mainstream Mysticism', July 1973

101. *PUBLIC SERVICE REVIEW* (South Australia), 'Elephant in the Dark' (by H. Houck), Adelaide, 1973

102. QUIGLY, ISABEL, 'Sufi to Say', *Sunday Telegraph*, 15 Jan 1967

103. *RADIO TIMES*, 'Idries Shah', 15 June 1971

104. *REGISTER-MAIL* (Galesburg, Ill.), 'Shah's Books Can be Read on Many Levels', 21 Oct 1970

105. REINKING, VIC, 'Ancient Teaching in Modern Setting', *Colorado Daily*, 25 Oct 1972

106. ROBSON, JIM, 'Essences of the East', *Irish Times*, 22 April 1968

107. SEMA ZAKI, 'Idries Shah/Contemporary Thinker of the East', *Culture Weekly* (Althaqafa Alasbua), 14 Oct 1972 (Damascus)

108. SEN, B. K., 'An Indian Philosopher', *Sunday World* (Delhi), 11 March 1973

109. SESHADRI, K., 'Sufi Thought', *The Hindu* (Madras), 13 Apr 1969

110. SEWELL, GORDON, 'Eastern Wisdom with Charm and Humour', *Southern Echo*, 24 Apr 1972

111. SIMAC, RAOUL, 'In a Naqshbandi Circle', *The Hibbert Journal*, Spring 1967

112. SMITH, STEVIE, 'Secrets of Good and Evil', *The Observer*, 1 Nov 1964

113. SPENCE, W. D., 'Stimulant', *Northern Echo*, 8 Sep 1970

114. *SUNDAY TELEGRAPH*, 'Sufi Subtleties', 15 March 1970

115. THOMSON, R. L., 'Psychology and Science from the Ancient East', *The Brook Postgraduate Gazette*, March 1973

116. *TIMES, THE*, 'The Computer Insists' (Letter), 5 Feb 1972

117. *TIMES, THE*, 'Sayed Idries Shah appointed guest professor', 18 May 1972, Court Circular page

118. *TIMES LITERARY SUPPLEMENT, THE*, On *Destination Mecca*: 19 June 1969; On *The Dermis Probe*: 7 Aug 1970; On *Thinkers of the East*: 7 May 1971

119. TOPSFIELD, ANDREW, '*The Way of the Sufi*, by Idries Shah', *Theoria to Theory*, April 1969

120. VANRENEN, D., 'Sufism: You Get Out of It what is in it for You', *Argus* (Cape Town), 26 Oct 1972

121. WADE, DAVID, 'Radio' (Idries Shah and an interview), *The Times*, 19 June 1971

122. 'WARWICK', 'Success Story', *The Courier*, Tunbridge Wells, 27 Dec 1968

123. WILD, THE REV. ERIC, *The Inquirer*, 'Mostly Blank', 21 Feb 1970; 'To gain True Wisdom', 1 Mar 1969; 'Sufficient Wisdom', 12 Dec 1970

124. WILLIAMS, PROF. L. F. RUSHBROOK, 'The Magic Monastery', *Asian Affairs*, Oct 1972

125. WILLIAMS, PAT, 'Nasrudin Moves in', *New Society*, 10 Nov 1966

126. WILLIAMS, PAT, 'Strong Doses of Truth',
     Sunday Times, 26 Nov 1967
127. WILSON, COLIN, 'Worlds of Magic',
     Books & Bookmen, June 1972
128. YALMAN, DR A. E., 'An Islamic Celebrity
     in English Cultural Life', *Bayram Gazetesi*
     (Istanbul), 22 July 1971

ALSO BY IDRIES SHAH

WISDOM OF THE IDIOTS
'Rare examples of non-linear thinking'
Evening News

CARAVAN OF DREAMS
'More than rewarding and impossible to
forget' *Tribune*

DESTINATION MECCA
'Intensely interesting' *The Spectator*

REFLECTIONS
'Tremendous application for *NOW*' *Review
of the Year*, BBC/4

ORIENTAL MAGIC
'A serious work of considerable
anthropological interest' *Contemporary
Review*

THE DERMIS PROBE
'Like a peepshow into a world which
most people do not imagine exists' *The
Guardian*

THE MAGIC MONASTERY
'A textbook for students... particularly
intriguing and informative' *Encounter*

THE BOOK OF THE BOOK
'Among other things an extraordinary
psychological test' *Sunday Telegraph*

THINKERS OF THE EAST
'Directly instructive' *Psychology Today*

TALES OF THE DERVISHES
'A jewel in the market place' *Sunday Times*

THE SUFIS
'The most sensible men on earth' *The
Listener*

THE EXPLOITS OF THE
INCOMPARABLE MULLA NASRUDIN
'It's a rare book that leaves the receptive
reader a *happier* but a wiser man!' *Books &
Bookmen*

THE PLEASANTRIES OF THE
INCREDIBLE MULLA NASRUDIN
'Undebased wisdom–an extension of the
proverbial' *Country Life*

THE WAY OF THE SUFI
'A present for anyone who, though religious,
finds the current orthodoxies unpalatable'
The Times Literary Supplement

THE SUBTLETIES OF THE INIMITABLE
MULLA NASRUDIN
'Mind-blowing... very, very good company,
an unexpected encounter I wouldn't have
missed but almost did' *Los Angeles Times*

Notes and Bibliography

WHERE POSSIBLE, CITATIONS have been made of European, American and other comparatively available works. All dates expressed in Christian Era terms.

1   Tholuck, F. A. G., *Sufismus sive Theosophia Persarum pantheistica*, Berlin 1821. (In Latin.)

2   Masonic rituals, words, terms, etc., can often be 'decoded' by using Sufi systems. For instances and references see my *The Sufis* (New York and London 1964, 1966; London 2015): 1964, 1966, pp. xix, 50, 178, 179, 182, 183, 184, 186, 188; 2015, pp. 61, 216, 217, 221, 222, 223, 226, 228. According to tradition (English citation in Brown, J. P., *The Darvishes*, London, p. 229, 1927 edn), the Sufi Masons have a warrant

from the Grand Lodge of Tiberias, whose members fled there from the destruction of Jerusalem. They became widely known in the Near East through Zounoun (Dhu'Nun), died 860.

3   Sufism: The word *Sufi* became current about 1,000 years ago, according to the 15th century poet and Sufi master, Jami (in his *Nafahat el-Uns*). Sheikh Suhrawardi dates it to the 9th century, and the word is not sufficiently established to be found in dictionaries of such a comparatively early date. Imam Qushairi in his *Rasail* places the appearance of the word in about 822. Earlier Sufis used many names, including The Kindred, The Recluses, The Virtuous, The Near Ones.

4   E.g., in Ibn Masarra of Cordoba (Spain), 883–931. For Sufic influence in Europe see, e.g., Garcin de Tassy, Introduction to the *Mantic-Uttair* (Parliament of the Birds), Paris 1864.

5   *Suf* = wool. Externalists in the East and West have often adopted this etymology, which therefore often appears in reference books as the derivation.

6   'Wool is the garb of animals' (*As-Suf libas al-Inam*), Arabic quotation from Hujwiri's

Revelation of the Veiled, in Sirdar Ikbal Ali Shah's *Islamic Sufism*, London 1933, p. 17.

7   This and other derivations have been used by Sufis themselves, explaining that 'bench' is not the original word, but the nearest equivalence which the Companions could find to their own word for themselves.

8   Higher functions of the mind: e.g., the Persian couplet '*Ba Murshid beshudi Insan/ Be Murshid mandi Haiwan*' ('With a Guide you may become a real man, without one you will remain an animal'); and Rumi: 'From realm to realm man went, reaching his present reasoning, knowledgeable, robust state – forgetting earlier forms of intelligence. So, too, shall he pass beyond the current forms of perception... There are a thousand other forms of Mind...' (Couplets of Inner Meaning, *Mathnavi-i-Maanavi*), and 'The degree of necessity determines the development of organs in man... Therefore increase your necessity.' (*Ibid.*)

9   *Jewish Encyclopaedia*, Vol. XI, pp. 579, 580, 581, *et passim*. Jewish sages regarded by Western scholars as following the Spanish Sufi schools include: Juda Halevi of Toledo, in his *Cuzari*, Moses ben Ezra of Granada, Josef ben Zadiq of Cordoba, in his

Microcosmus, Samuel ben Tibbón, Simtob ben Falaquera.

10 Identity of Sufi ideas with ancient Egyptian, Pythagorean and Platonic noted, e.g., by Ubicini, M. A., *Letters on Turkey*, London 1856.

11 'Theosophy' used of Sufism: see Tholuck, op. cit. (item [1] above). This book appeared ten years before Mme Blavatsky was born, and nine years before the birth of Col. Olcott, co-founder of the Theosophical Society.

12 Nicholson, R. A., *The Mystics of Islam*, London 1914, pp. 3–4. Professor Nicholson was in his time believed to be a great authority on Sufism and published several useful books and translations. 'Nicholson was the greatest authority on Islamic mysticism this country has produced, and in his own considerable field was the supreme authority in the world.' (*The Times*, 27 August 1945)

13 Nicholson, R. A., *The Kashf al-Mahjub* (Revelation of the Veiled), London 1911, p. 34.

14 *The Persian Sufis*, London 1964, p. 9. Increasing Roman Catholic interest in Sufism, already shown to have had a significant ancient effect upon Catholic mystics and academicians, is recently evidenced

by the fact that this book was given *Nihil Obstat* and the *Imprimatur* of the Dominican and Diocesan authorities of Rome. Its author believes that the future purpose of Sufism will be 'to make possible a welding of religious thought between East and West, a vital oecumenical commingling and understanding, which will prove ultimately to be, in the truest sense, on both sides, a return to origins, to the original unity' (*ibid.*, p. 10).

15 Summed up by the Sufi ancient Abdul-Aziz Mekki (died 652) as 'Offer a donkey a salad, and he will ask you what kind of a thistle it is.'

16 *The Sufis*, New York and London 1964, 1966; London 2015.

17 Asín Palacios, Professor Miguel, *Un precursor hispanomusulman de San Juan de la Cruz*; in Andulus I, pp. 7ff., 1933. And see: Nwyia, P., *Ibn Abbad de Ronda et Jean de la Croix*; in Andulus 22, pp. 113ff., 1957.

18 Asín: *El Simil de los Castillos y moradas del alma en mistica islamica y en Santa Teresa*; in Andulus II, pp. 263 ff., 1946.

19 *The Sufis*, New York and London 1964, 1966, p. 239; London 2015, p. 246; and Baron Carra de Vaux in *Journal Asiatique*, vol. 19, p. 63. The Franciscan Roger Bacon

(died 1294), wearing Arab dress, discoursed at Oxford, quoting the Hikmat el-Ishraq (*Wisdom of Illumination*) identified with the Sufi school of Sheikh Shahabudin Yahya Suhrawardi, who had been executed for apostasy and carrying on 'the ancient philosophy' in 1191. For Franciscan connection with Sufism, see *The Sufis*.

20 *The Sufis*, New York and London 1964, 1966, pp. xvi, 155, 191, 194, 196, 199, 202–4, 243, 370; London 2015, pp. 188, 232, 235, 246, 248, 295, 447.

21 Asin: *Abenmasarra*; and *The Sufis*, New York and London 1964, 1966, pp. xvii, xix, 42, 140, 203–5, 243, 244, 246, 247, 261, 370, 388, 389; London 2015, pp. 52, 170, 246, 247, 248, 249, 294, 295, 296, 299, 300, 316, 447, 469; Ribera, J., *Origines de la Filosofia de Raimundo Lulio*.

22 Loehlin, C. F., 'Sufism and Sikhism', *Moslem World* 29, pp. 351ff., 1939; and see: *The Sufis*, New York and London 1964, 1966, pp. 358f.; London 2015, p. 433.

23 Swan, C., *Gesta Romanorum*, London 1829, etc. The first known Western manuscript of this collection dates from 1324. Its stories are found in Shakespeare's *King Lear*, *The Merchant of Venice*, *Pericles*, *The Rape of*

Lucrece. Chaucer, Lydgate and Boccacio all
included material from this source.

24 Barth, A., *Religions of India*; Dr Tara Chand
    in *The Cultural History of India*, Hyderabad
    1958, p. 153; and *The Sufis*, New York and
    London 1964, 1966, pp. 356ff; London
    2015, p. 432.

25 See my *The Secret Lore of Magic*, London
    1957, 1963, 1965, 2016 and New York
    1958. For the Sufi attitude to magic, see *The
    Sufis*, New York and London 1964, 1966,
    pp. 326ff.; London 2015, pp. 394ff.; and
    my *Destination Mecca*, London 1957, pp.
    169ff; 2016, pp. 218ff. For supernormal
    faculties exercised by Sufis, see J. P. Brown's
    The Darvishes, London 1867 (and 1927 ed.
    by Rose); L. M. J. Garnett's *Mysticism and
    Magic in Turkey*, London 1912; S. A. Salik's
    The Saint of Gilan, Lahore 1953 and 1961;
    J. A. Subhan's *Sufism – its Saints and Shrines*,
    Lucknow 1939.

26 Freud's psychological symbolism interpre-
    tation method is used in the Sufi Ghazali's
    Niche, 900 years before Freud: see (s.v.
    Symbolism) in Gairdner's translation of the
    Niche, Royal Asiatic Society, London 1924
    (reprinted in *Four Sufi Classics*, London
    1980). The 'Jüngian Archetypal theory'

was known to Sufis in ancient times: see Prof. R. Landau's *The Philosophy of Ibn Arabi*, New York 1959, p. 4ff. Freud's debt to Kabbalism and Jewish mysticism, which Jewish authorities regard as derived from Sufism or identical with it, is treated in Professor David Bakan's *Sigmund Freud and the Jewish Mystical Tradition*, New York 1958.

27 Certain reviewers and others, ignorant of the fact that Sufi books seldom have indices (so that the reader will read the book in its entirety), have deplored the lack of an index to *The Sufis*. The Coombe Springs Press issued an independent Index to *The Sufis* in 1965.

28 E. W. F. Tomlin, FRAS, *Great Philosophers of the East*, London 1959, p. 295.

29 *Great Philosophers of the West*.

30 London 1959 and 1960.

31 Some experts' opinions about the 'origins' of Sufism: 'The influence of Christian mysticism is paramount' (Prof. E. W. F. Tomlin, *Great Philosophers of the East*, London 1959, p. 295). 'A reaction from the burdens of a dry monotheism, of a rigid law and a stiffened ritual' (Rev. Dr Sell, *Sufism*, Madras 1910 p. 11). '...Having its origins in the

religious conceptions of India and Greece'
(Brown, J. P., *ibid.*, 1927, p. v). 'Appear to
be a kind of Gnostics' (Redhouse, J. W.,
The Mesnevi, London 1881, p. xiv). '...the
emotional character of Sufism, so different
from the cold and bloodless theories of the
Indian philosophies, is apparent' (Prof. E.
G. Browne, *A Lit. Hist. of Persia*, London
1909, p. 442). '...a little Persian sect' (Had-
land Davis, F., *The Persian Mystics: Jalalu-
ddin Rumi*, London 1907, p. 1). '...great
perversion of Mohammad's teaching' (Bell,
Miss G. L., *Poem from the Divan of Hafiz*,
London 1928, p. 51). 'Derived in part from
Plato, "the Attic Moses", but mainly from
Christianity' (Whinfield, E. H., *Masnavi i
ma'navi, the Spiritual Couplets*, London
1887, p. xv). 'Orientalists ... have indeed
attributed the origins of Sufism to Persian,
Hindu, Neo Platonic or Christian sources.
But these diverse attributions have ended by
cancelling one another' (Burckhardt, T., *An
Introduction to Sufi Doctrine*, tr. Matheson,
D. M., Lahore, Pakistan 1959, p. 5).

32 Nicholson, R. A., Selections from the
Diwan-i-Shams-i-Tabriz, Cambridge 1988
and 1952, pp. xxxvi ff. Professor Edward
Palmer has recorded for Western students

the fact that *Mutrib*, the Arabic equivalent of Troubadour, also stands for 'Sufi teacher' (*Oriental Mysticism*, p. 80). Professor Hitti is even more explicit: 'In southern France the first Provençal poets appear full-fledged towards the end of the 11th century with palpitating love expressed in a wealth of fantastic imagery. The troubadours (*Tarab*: music, song) who flourished in the 12th century imitated their southern contemporaries, the *zajal* singers. Following the Arabic precedent the cult of the dame suddenly arises in south-west Europe. The *Chanson de Roland*, the noblest of early European literature, whose appearance prior to 1080 marks the beginning of a new civilisation – that of Western Europe – just as the Homeric poems mark the beginning of historic Greece, owes its existence to a military contact with Moslem Spain.' (Hitti, P. K., *History of the Arabs*, 1951 edition, p. 562)

33 William Tell Legend: see Robert Graves' Introduction to *The Sufis* (item 2, above, 1964 and 1966, p. xvii; the Graves introduction was not included in later editions). The most accessible English rendering of Attar's *Bird Parliament* is the 1954 version,

translated by C. S. Nott from a French copy, reissued in 1961, in London. The Rev. Baring-Gould had shown in Victorian times the Tell legend lacked historical backing. Hadyn's *Dictionary of Dates* says: 'The popular stories respecting him were demonstrated to be mythical by Professor Kopf of Lucerne, 1872' (s.v. 'Tell').

34 Peacock Angel cult: founded by the Sufi master Sheikh Adi ben Musafir (died 1162). A chapter on this society is to be found in Arkon Daraul's *Secret Societies* (Chapter 15), London 1961 and 1965, published in New York in 1961 as *A History of Secret Societies*. The symbolology of the cult can be unlocked by applying the 'Abjad-notation' encipherment system used by the Sufis, described in *The Sufis*; extensively used by poets and Sufis. See also Note 92.

35 G. I. Gurdjieff left abundant clues to the Sufic origins of virtually every point in his 'system'; though it obviously belongs more specifically to the Khajagan (Naqshbandi) form of the dervish teaching. In addition to the practices of 'the work', such books as Gurdjieff's *Beelzebub* (otherwise known as *All and Everything*, New York 1950, 1,238 pages) and *Meetings with Remarkable*

Men, 2nd impression, 1963, abound with references, often semi-covert ones, to the Sufi system. He also cites by name the Naqshbandis, Kubravis and other Sufis, in his 1923 Paris 'prospectus' of a public presentation (*The Echo of the Champs-Elysees*, 1, 37, part 2, Paris: 13–25 Dec. 1923) quoting as sources, *inter alia*, the Naqshbandi, Qadiri, Kalandar, Kubravi and Mevlevi dervish practices. Maurice Nicoll's *Psychological Commentaries* (London 1952, 1953, 1957) and *The New Man* (London 1950) abound with examples of Sufic methods used to interpret religious and other documents. These works depart from Sufi usage in dealing with subjects in a random fashion, and being aimed at an 'accidental' rather than a chosen community of students. P. D. Ouspensky: largely through his contact with G. I. Gurdjieff, this Russian philosopher names the Sufis as a source of ancient psychology, e.g., in *The Psychology of Man's Possible Evolution*, London 1951, p. 7. Ouspensky, however, had no direct contact with dervishes and was unable to effect the necessary transposition of Sufic ideas from their literary sources in Eastern and other literature into the terminology used in his 'system'. Had he been able to do so, he would have realised that his 'system' had ignored the Sufi requirements of 'time, place and certain people'. He attempts to systematise the material of Gurdjieff in *In Search of the Miraculous*, London 1950, etc., in which he records conversations with Gurdjieff. Both the Naqshbandi Sufis and the Gurdjieff-Ouspenskians call their studies 'The Fourth Way' (*The Fourth Way*, Ouspensky, London 1957).

36   *Hammerskjöld and Sufis*: Jalaludin Rumi, quoted literally by him (*Markings*, London 1964, p. 95); and see also *Reader's Digest* quoting (*Dagens Nyheter*, Stockholm, 1962) his copy of the Sufi poem translated by Sir William Jones (1746–94): 'On parent knees, a naked newborn child/Weeping thou sat'st while all around thee smiled/So live, that sinking in thy last long sleep/Calm thou may'st smile while all around thee weep'; and see his *Markings*, *passim*.

37   Shakespeare's plays not only contain many stories of Persian, Arabian and other Eastern origins, but what might seem almost literal quotations from Sufi literature. Prof. Nicholson has noted one or two equivalents from the *Divan of Shams-i-Tabriz*, in his

translation of that book (see Note 32 above), on pp. 290 and 291 (*et passim*). See also Garcin de Tassy's *Philosophical and Religious Poetry of the Persians*, Paris 1864.

38 Professor Kenneth Walker, *Diagnosis of Man*, London 1962, quoted the Sanai-Rumi Sufi school usage of the legend of the 'Elephant in the Dark', to show how modern man may fumble with parts of a problem, instead of going to the heart of it. Walker follows Gurdjieff; vide his *Study of Gurdjieff's Teaching*.

39 The 'Tale of the Ugly Duckling' is one, vide *The Sufis*.

40 Hitchman, F., *Burton*, I, p. 286.

41 By L. A. Hill.

42 E.g. Saxe, J. G., *The Blind Men and the Elephant*, London 1964; and Downing, C. (tr.), *Tales of the Hodja*, London 1964.

43 *The Sufis*, New York and London 1964, 1966, pp. 208ff., 243; London 2015, pp. 253ff., 295. Eastern origins of 'witches': Bracelin, J. L., *Gerald Gardner – Witch*, London 1960, p. 75; and Daraul, A., *Witches and Sorcerers*, New York 1966, pp. 20, 23–4; 73, 204f., *et passim*.

44 Rosicrucians' origins: see *The Sufis*, New York and London 1964, 1966, pp. 187, 191,

223, 389f.; London 2015, pp. 227, 232, 272, 470f., and Daraul, A., *Secret Societies*. Rosicrucians claim that their founder brought his knowledge from Arabia, Fez and Egypt. The origins have been traced by Daraul, *ibid*. p. 195, to the Qadiri Sufi Order.

45 Daraul, A., *Secret Societies*, London 1961, ch. 22; Jurji, E. J., *The Illuministic Sufis*, JAOS 57, pp. 90ff., 1937; and Brown, *Darvishes*, London 1868, republished (ed. Rose) London 1927.

46 See *The Sufis*, *passim*, for references to the influence of Ghazali and others on Western Europe. Most books on mediaeval scholasticism and the history of its thought carry references to this source. Cf. Professor P. Hitti's *History of the Arabs* (Note 29 above); and G. Leff's *Mediaeval Thought*, London 1958.

47 See, for instance, O. B. Kapor's *Research Thesis on the Mystic Philosophy of Kabir* (Allahabad University Studies 10, p. 166, 1933).

48 Ivanow, W., *The Truth Worshippers of Kurdistan*, Leiden 1953, pp. 57–68 *et passim*.

49 The people who became known as the Assassins were a Sufi organisation originally

called *Asasin* ('People of the Foundation, the Fundamentals'), a branch of which was taken over in the 10th Christian century by Hasan, son of Sabah, known as the Great Assassin or Old Man of the Mountains. This name is a mistranslation of his usurped title, *Sheikh el-Jabal* (Master of the Mountains) erroneously rendered by Westerners in its alternative meaning '(Sheikh) of Senex del Monte', which Crusaders called him. The 'Aga Khans' are reputed to be descended from this Hasan. Another, rival, leader of the cult is located in Bombay. The original 'order', however, continues independently. Vide: Sirdar Ikbal Ali Shah, 'The General Principles of Sufism', in *Hibbert Journal*, vol. 20 (1921–22), pp. 523–35. Great confusion has been created in the West by literal translation of Arabic names. Hence, for instance, while 'Algazel' may be seen to be Al-Ghazali, not everyone recognises 'Doctor Maximus' (The Greatest Teacher) as El-Sheikh el-Akbar (Ibn Arabi); or 'Basil Valentine' (The Triumphant King) as El-Malik el-Fatih, the alchemist; or, for that matter, the anti-witch tract *Errores Gaziorum* as 'Ghulat aljazair' (Sects of Algeria).

50 Examples, etc., relating to Zen, *The Sufis*, New York and London 1964, 1966, pp. 309, 362–4; London 2015, pp. 374, 438–40.

51 See *The Sufis*, New York and London 1964, 1966, p. 309; London 2015, p. 374. Yoga and Zen material nowadays tends to ignore the special requirements of choice of disciple and type of teacher.

52 Knights Templar: *ibid.*, 1964, 1966, pp. xiv, xix, 225–7, 399; 2015, pp. 274–6.

53 Chaucer: *ibid.*, 1964, 1966, pp. xxii, 50, 104, 106, 115, 163, 166, 223, 393; 2015, pp. 61, 126, 129, 141, 197, 202, 272, 474.

54 Prof. M. Asín Palacios: *Islam and the Divine Comedy* (Ibn el-Arabi, 1165–1240), tr. H. Sunderland, London 1926 (*La Escatologia Musulmana en la Divina Comedia*, Madrid, 1961).

55 For instance, in Munaqib el-Arifin (*The Acts of the Adepts*), by Shamsudin Ahmad el-Aflaki, tr. Redhouse, London 1881; reprinted facsimile, Kingston (as *Legends of the Sufis*) 1965, pp. 35f. And see: Ghazali, *Alchemy of Happiness*.

56 Rumi (1207–73) was born in Balkh, Afghanistan, and died at Konia (Iconium), Turkey, where 'dervish dancing' in public is now proscribed except as a tourist spectacle.

57 Died 1949.

58 Died 1947.

59 Abdul-Qadir of Gilan ('Sultan of the Friends'), 1077–1166; Hadrat Bahaudin Naqshband (El-Shah), 1318–1389.

60 'Truth comes after "states" and ecstasy, and takes its place.' Kalabadhi, *Kitab el-Taaruf* (in A. J. Arberry's version, *The Doctrine of the Sufis*, Cambridge 1935, p. 106: 'But when Truth cometh, ecstasy itself is dispossessed'), citing Junaid of Baghdad (died 910).

61 Founded by an Indonesian, Mohammed Subuh, in 1934. Indiscriminate indulgence in the *Latihan* exercise has been known to give rise to a condition referred to in medical literature as 'Subud psychosis'.

62 In *Fihi Ma Fihi* (Professor A. J. Arberry's translation, London 1961, entitled *Discourses of Rumi*); *The Mathnawi* (translations of R. A. Nicholson, London 1926; J. W. Redhouse, London 1881; E. H. Whinfield, London 1887 and 1898; C. E. Wilson, London 1910, etc.).

63 First Book of the *Hadiqa* (Walled Garden of Truth), Calcutta 1910, tr. Maj. J. Stephenson; *Karnama* ('Book of the Work'), and *Diwan*.

64 *Niche for Lamps* – Mishkat al-Anwar (tr. W. H. T. Gairdner, London 1924, Royal

Asiatic Society); and Lahore (Pakistan), 1952; reprinted in *Four Sufi Classics*, London 1980. *Ihya el Ulum el-Din* (Revival of Religious Sciences).

65 *Futuhat al-Makkia* (*Openings in Mecca*); *Fusus el-Hikam* (*Bezels of the Wisdoms*); *Kimia-i-Sadat* (*Alchemy of Happiness*); *Tarjuman el-Ashwaq* (*Interpreter of Desires*, tr. Nicholson).

66 See: Dietrici, *Der Darwinismus in 10 und 19 Jahrhundert*, Leipzig 1879; and: *Mathnavi*.

67 Shabistari, *Garden of Mysteries/Secret Garden* (13th–14th centuries), Sayed Ahmad Isfahani, *Tarjiband*, and others.

68 E.g.: 'The Hidden World has clouds and rain, of a different kind... made apparent only to the refined, those not deceived by the seeming completeness of the ordinary world' (Rumi, *Mathnavi*):

> *Ghaib ra abri wa abi digar ast*
> *Asman wa aftab-i-digar ast.*
> *Nayad an ilia ki bar pakan padid*
> *Barqiyan fi labs min khalkin jadid.*

69 E.g. in Hujwiri's (11th century) *Revelation of the Veiled*, s.v. 'Recapitulation of their Miracles'.

70   See, for example, No. IX in Nicholson's *Divan of Shamsi-Tabriz*, p. 32 (13th century), Persian text.

71   *La Quintessence de la Philosophie de Ibn-i-Arabi* (Prof. Mohammed Ali Aini, tr. A. Rechid), Paris 1926, pp. 66–7.

72   Junaid of Baghdad (died 910) answered conditioned minds thus: 'None reaches the rank of Truth until a thousand honest people testify that he is a heretic.'

73   Arabic: *Al-turuqu illahi ka nufusi bani Adama* (in *Islamic Sufism* – Note 6 above, p. 211).

74   See, e.g., Saadi's *Gulistan* (Rose Garden) of the 13th century: section on Manners of the Dervishes, Agha Omar Ali-Shah's translation, *Gulistan* (Sheikh Muslihuddin Saadi Shirazi, *Le Jardin de Roses*), Paris 1966; and cf. Ibn Hamdan, cited in Hujwiri's *Kashf*: 'Be sure that you do not train yourself to music, in case this holds you back from even higher perceptions.' Contemporary dervishes of the Chishti 'order' have strayed far from the instructions of their founder in this matter, settling for a dissociated or ecstatic state induced by listening to or playing music. Muinudin Chishti himself wrote against this practice: 'They know that we listen to music

and that we perceive certain "secrets" as a result. So they play music and cast themselves into "states". Know that every learning must have all its requirements fulfilled, not just music, thought, concentration. Remember: what is the good of a wonderful milk yield from a cow which kicks the pail over?' (Risalat, *Epistles to Disciples*)

75 Although all pay lip-service to the teachings of Ibn-Arabi, for instance, they have not absorbed such words as these: 'She has confused all the learned of Islam/All who have studied the Psalms/Every Jewish Rabbi/ Every Christian Priest', where he refers to Sufism. Or the famous words of Abu-Said ibn Abu'l Khair (1040): 'Until college and minaret have crumbled/This holy work of ours will not be done. Until faith becomes rejection, and rejection becomes belief/There will be no true Moslem.' On the limitations of religious 'vehicle': 'What can I do, O Moslems? I do not know myself. I am no Christian, no Jew, no Magian, no Musulman. Not of the East, nor of the West.' (*Divan of Shams-i-Tabriz*, reprint of Nicholson, London 1911, xxxii, p. 124 Persian version)

76 Ibn el-Arabi, *Fusus el-Hikam* (Bezels or Segments of the Wisdoms), s.v. El-Fas

el-Adamia ('Segment of Adam') paraphrased in S. A. Q. Husaini's *Ibn Al Arabi*, Lahore 1931 edition; French version: Burkhardt, T., *La Sagesse des Prophetes*, Paris 1955, pp. 22f.

77 Birge, Dr J. K., *The Bektashi Order of Dervishes*, London 1937, p. 39, note 3 (reprinted 1965).

78 Brown, J. P., *The Darvishes* (ed. H. A. Rose), London 1927, p. 475.

79 These cults are sometimes deteriorations of such communities as I describe in *Destination Mecca*, London 1957, pp. 169ff; London 2016, pp. 218ff.

80 A penetrating perception of the fact that many Sufi ideas have filtered into primitive communities was written by the well-known poet Ted Hughes two years ago: 'One would almost be inclined to say that Shamanism might well be a barbarised, stray descendant of Sufism.' (*The Listener*, London, 29 October 1964, p. 678)

(80A) Lawrence, P., *Road Belong Cargo*, London 1964, contains a description of this cult and has an excellent bibliography.

81 *Blackwood's Magazine*, Vol. 290, No. 1754, pp. 481–595; and Vol. 291, No. 1756, pp. 123–35.

82 *Siraat* (English-language), Delhi, Vol. 1, No. 5, 1 January 1961, p. 5, cols 1–3, 'Sufism in a Changing World', by Selim Brook-White, 'Murid'.

83 *International Journal of Clinical and Experimental Hypnosis*, Vol. 10, No. 4 (October), pp. 271–4: Hallaj, J., *Hypnotherapeutic Techniques in a Central Asian Community*. Reprinted 1965 in Shor, R. E., and Orne, M. T., *The Nature of Hypnosis* (Selected Basic Readings), New York, V. 6, pp. 453ff.

84 *Contemporary Review* (London), Vol. 197, No. 1132, May 1960: Foster, W., *The Family of Hashim*, pp. 269–71.

85 *The Lady* (London), Vol. CLXII, No. 4210, 9 Dec 1965: Martin, D. R., *Below the Hindu Kush*, p. 870.

(85A) Some of these articles are now reprinted in Davidson, R. W., *Documents on Contemporary Dervish Communities*, London 1966 and 1967.

86 *The Times* (London), No. 55,955, 9 March 1964, 'Elusive Guardians of Ancient Secrets', p. 12, cols 6–8.

87 *She* magazine (London), March 1963, p. 58: ('She Looks at Religion – No. 11'); and also: *She* magazine (London), September 1965,

'The Hard High Life', by Mir S. Khan, pp. 68–70. (Both items illustrated.)

88   From Ghazali's monumental *Revival of Religious Sciences*.

89   Sentences upon Sufis and Sufism by early historical masters of the Sufis:

Dhun'Nun the Egyptian (died 860): 'A Sufi is one whose speech accords with his behaviour and whose silence indicates his state, and who discards wordly connections.'

The woman adept Rabia el-Adawia (died 717): 'The Sufi is he who neither fears hell nor covets paradise.'

Abul-Hasan Nuri (died 907): 'Sufism is the renunciation of all pleasures of the (transitory) world.'

Hujwiri (11th century): 'The follower of Sufism is he who seeks to reach the rank of being dead to self and alive to truth by means of struggle. He who has reached this end is called a Sufi.'

Junaid of Baghdad (died 910): 'Sufism is an attribute wherein is man's subsistence.'

Nuri: 'The Sufi has no possession, nor is he possessed by anything.'

Ibn el-Lalali (11th century): 'Sufism is truth without formulation.'

90 Rumi, 'AQL' = real intellect, NB. Rumi: 'The Sufi's book is not literacy and letters.'

91 This is how psychological and other diagrams become 'mandalas' and 'magic figures'.

(91A) Various versions of the dervish teaching-stories in my *Tales of the Dervishes* (London 1967, 2016) have been represented by Sufi masters as events which happened to them, for this reason.

92 As Professor A. J. Arberry of Cambridge puts it, the doctrine is obscure because it is 'based largely on experiences in their very nature well nigh incommunicable' (*Tales from the Masnavi*, London 1961, p. 19). The technical term for one form of this, the use of words written similarly which have different meanings, is *Jinas-i-Mukharij*, much used in poetry. Gibb (*History of Ottoman Poetry*, I, 118, 1900) shows familiarity with this system, but fails to apply it in his studies.

93 Mahmud Shabistari (1317), in common with many other Sufi teachers, speaks thus of the transient nature of formulation: 'If the Moslem knew what an idol was/He would know that there is religion in idolatry./If the

idolater knew what religion was:/He would know where he had gone astray./He sees in the idol nothing but the obvious creature:/This is why, in Islamic Law, he is a heathen.' (*Gulshan-i-Raz, Garden of Secrets.*) Persian text: 'Musulman gar bi-danist ki but chist/ Bi-danisti ki din dar butparasti'st./Agar mushrik zi din agah gashti/Kuja dar din i khud gumrah gashti./Na did u dar but illa khalqi zahir:/Badan illat shud an dar Shara, Kafir.'

94   How little this important part of Sufi transmission is known in 'the literature of the field' is evidenced by the fact that almost the only reference to humour in Sufism at all current is made by an American student (Dr J. K. Birge: *The Bektashi Order of Dervishes*, London 1937, p. 88); and even he regards it as a 'characteristic peculiarity' of the Order which he is studying. See also my *The Exploits of the Incomparable Mulla Nasrudin*, London 1966, 2014.

95   The best-known case is that of Husain ibn Mansur el-Hallaj, the great Sufi martyr, dismembered alive and done to death, his corpse then being burnt, by the order of the Caliph el-Muqtadir, of the House of Haroun

el-Rashid, in the year 922, for allegedly claiming that he was God. Professor Louis Massignon has specialised in the Hallaj literature. See also Note 100, below. The great teacher Suhrawardi, too, was executed for teaching 'ancient philosophy' in the 12th century (see Note 19, above).

(95A) On conditioned and indoctrinated groups and movements, see Liftan, R. J., *Thought Reform*, London 1961; Mann J., *Changing Human Behaviour*, New York 1965; Sprott W. J. H., *Human Groups*, London 1958, 1962, 1963; *Small Social Groups in England*, Phillips, M., London 1965.

96 The story of how Uwais was visited by Companions of Mohammed after the Prophet's death is found in many books, including the well-known *Recital of the Friends* (Lives of the Saints) by Faridudin Attar, translated as *Le Memorial des Saints*, by A. Pavet de Courteille and published in Paris in 1889 (pp. 11f.). See Dr B. Behari's English abridgement (*Fariduddin Attar's Tadhkiratal-Auliya*), Lahore, Pakistan 1961 and 1965.

97 The *Awarif-ul-Ma'rif* written in the 13th century by Sheikh Shahabudin Umar ibn

Mohamed Suhrawardi, version of Mahmud ibn Ali Alkashani, translated from Persian into English by Col. H. Wilberforce Clarke, Calcutta 1890.

98 Died 1234. Literally the passage runs in Arabic: Sharibna ala dhikri alhabibi mudamatu/Shakirna bi ha min qabli an yukhlaka alkarmu. Professor Hitti (op. cit., p. 436) calls Ibn el Farid the only Arab mystical poet.

99 Wilberforce Clarke's rendering, see *supra*, Note 97.

100 See Prof. L. Massignon's *Le Diwan d'Al Hallaj*, Paris 1955, etc.

101 See his *Turkish Nationalism and Western Civilisation*, London 1959.

102 E.g., Ibn el-Arabi's dictum: 'People think that a Sheikh should show miracles and manifest illumination. The requirement of a teacher is, however, that he should possess all that the disciple needs.'

103 Recorded in Hujwiri's *Revelation of the Veiled*.

104 *Munaqib*, as quoted, Note 56, above.

105 He wrote *Majma el-Bahrain* ('Confluence of the Two Seas') published in translation by the Asiatic Soc. of Bengal.

SPECIAL PROBLEMS

106 In a Sufi circle, even one unsuitable member will harm the effort of the whole; enunciated for instance by Saadi (1184–1263), in his *Gulistan* (Rose Garden), 'On the Manners of Dervishes'.

107 Omar Khayyam for considerations of the Khyamic Sufi teachings, see: Swami Govinda Tirtha's *The Nectar of Grace: Omar Khayyam's Life and Works*, Allahabad 1941; and cf. *The Sufis*, New York and London, 1964, 1966, pp. 164–71; London 2015, pp. 199–208. The poem quoted is Quatrain 24 of the Bodleian MS, published by Heron-Allen (*The Ruba'iyat of Omar Khayyam*, London 1898). Text facsimile and translation on p. 141. The original text is:

> *Dar sauma'a wa madrasa wa deir wa kanisht –*
> *Tarsinda zi dozakhand wa juya-i-bihisht.*
> *Ankas ki zi asrar-i-khuda ba-khabar ast:*
> *Z'in tukhm dar andarun-i-dil hich nakasht.*

Khayyam's *Rubaiyat* was translated and published in 1967 by Robert Graves and Omar Ali Shah, with critical commentaries.

108 English version: Maulvi S. A. Q. Husaini, *Ibn Al Arabi*, Lahore 1931, VI, 1 (p. 38).

109 Simac, R., 'In a Naqshbandi Circle', *Hibbert Journal*, Spring 1967 (Vol. 65, No. 258). See also my *The Exploits of the Incomparable Mulla Nasrudin* (London and New York 1966; London 2014), and my *Caravan of Dreams* (London 1968, 2014).

Index

A Request

If you enjoyed this book, please review it on Amazon and Goodreads.

Reviews are an author's best friend.

To stay in touch with news on forthcoming editions of Idries Shah works, please sign up for the mailing list:

 http://bit.ly/ISFlist

And to follow him on social media, please go to any of the following links:

 https://twitter.com/idriesshah

 https://www.facebook.com/IdriesShah

 http://www.youtube.com/idriesshah999

 http://www.pinterest.com/idriesshah/

 http://bit.ly/ISgoodreads

 http://idriesshah.tumblr.com

 https://www.instagram.com/idriesshah/

http://idriesshahfoundation.org

Lightning Source UK Ltd.
Milton Keynes UK
UKHW010951060122
396715UK00001B/226